WORSHIPING
WITH
UNITED
METHODISTS

WORSHIPING WITH UNITED METHODISTS

A Guide for Pastors and Church Leaders

HOYT L. HICKMAN

Abingdon Press
Nashville

WORSHIPING WITH UNITED METHODISTS:
A GUIDE FOR PASTORS AND CHURCH LEADERS

Copyright © *1996 by Abingdon Press*

This book is printed on recycled, acid-free paper.

Library of Congress Cataloging-in-Publication Data

Hickman, Hoyt L. (Hoyt Leon), 1927–
    Worshiping with United Methodists: a guide for pastors and church leaders/Hoyt Leon Hickman.
        p.   cm.
    Includes bibliographical references.
    ISBN 0-687-00782-8 (alk. paper)
    1. Public worship—United Methodist Church (U.S.)   2. United Methodist Church (U.S.)—Liturgy.   3. Methodist Church—United States—Liturgy.   I. Title.
    BX8382.2.Z5H54   1996
    264'.076—dc20   95-49806
                                                                                         CIP

03 04 05—10 9 8

MANUFACTURED IN THE UNITED STATES OF AMERICA

CONTENTS

CHAPTER 1

Getting Started

✝

YOU, THE READER

This is a book for pastors and others who plan and lead worship in United Methodist congregations. You may be a student preparing for, or actually facing, your first appointment as pastor of a United Methodist congregation without previous experience in planning and leading congregational worship. Perhaps you may have attended worship in United Methodist congregations many times in your life, but without thinking much about how services are planned, let alone why they are as they are or how they could be improved. Or you may have little past experience of any kind of congregational worship.

Or you may be coming into a United Methodist pastorate from another denomination, either as a student or as an experienced pastor. You may wonder about United Methodist worship customs that seem strange to you.

Or you may be an experienced pastor who learned a certain way of planning and leading worship but are no longer content to do things the way you've always done them. You may have been appointed to a congregation whose worship traditions are different from those you are used to, or where you sense that the kind of worship you are used to planning and leading is not appropriate. Perhaps you have been at your present pastorate for some time but have a growing sense that the worship you have been planning and leading is not working very well. Even if your services seem to satisfy those who now attend, you may sense that something else is needed to meet the needs of others you ought to be reaching.

Or you may have been invited to work with your pastor in planning and leading services, occasionally or regularly. You may be an associate pastor, a diaconal minister, a church musician, a lay speaker or lay worship leader, or the worship chairperson. You may be on the worship committee or belong to the altar guild. Perhaps you sense that you would be a more effective member of the worship team if you knew more about worship.

Or you may be a concerned layperson. You feel that something needs to change if your congregation's worship is to come alive. Or you want to understand the changes you see taking place.

Whatever your role, somewhere you may have experienced worship that was **alive,** that moved you deeply to experience the presence of God and empower you for your daily life. You wish that services in your congregation each week could be like that. You want to know **why** some worship comes alive while other worship is boring, if not dead. And you want to know **how** to bring life to your worship.

YOUR RESOURCES

There are three basic resources for planning and leading worship in United Methodist congregations.

1) The Bible is both our primary authority and our primary worship resource. Reading the Bible and faithfully interpreting it through preaching and other means is primary in our worship. The prayer and praise with which we respond to God's Word gain added power when they use words of scripture. As we examine congregational worship, of prime

importance are its biblical basis and any biblical guidelines that apply.

2) *The United Methodist Hymnal*,[1] officially adopted by the 1988 General Conference of The United Methodist Church, is, together with the Bible, the people's book of worship. It contains a wealth of resources recommended for United Methodist congregations to read or sing in their worship. In the rest of this book it is referred to simply as the hymnal. The abbreviation *UMH*, followed by a number, indicates where an act of worship or a quotation is found in the hymnal.

3) *The United Methodist Book of Worship*,[2] officially adopted by the 1992 General Conference of The United Methodist Church, contains an additional wealth of resources for those who plan and lead congregational worship, with thousands of cross references to the Bible and to the hymnal. In the rest of this book it is referred to simply as the *Book of Worship*. The abbreviation *BOW*, followed by a number, indicates where an act of worship or a quotation is found in the *Book of Worship*.

Those who plan and lead worship in United Methodist congregations need to become familiar with all three of these basic resources. Since there are constant references to them in this book, you will find it very helpful to have all of them handy for reference as you continue reading this book.

You will also need additional resources as you plan services. Some are suggested at the back of this book. Others are outside the scope of this book but in related fields. This book is focused on the acts and structures of the Sunday service that are constant from week to week, but you will also need re-sources to help you and your congregation understand and observe the Christian Year. The Christian Year index in the back of the hymnal (937-38) and the Christian Year section of the *Book of Worship* (224-420) are basic for this purpose. Numerous collections of worship resources keyed to the days and seasons of the Christian Year are published each year and are widely advertised and available. Given the different wor-ship styles that they reflect, only you and your congregation

¶ *9*

can determine which will be helpful to you. One book, however, is specifically recommended because this book is designed to be used with it.

The New Handbook of the Christian Year[3] is a survey of the history, meaning, and practice of the Christian Year, including acts and services of worship for each of the days and seasons of the year. It does for the Christian Year what this book does for the constant elements of the Sunday service. The two books can well be used side by side.

Preaching resources, musical resources, and resources relating to other worship-related arts are obviously essential, as is education and training in the techniques and skills needed to use them.

Baptism, confirmation, and other services of the Baptismal Covenant (*UMH* 32-54; *BOW* 81-114) usually take place in the Sunday service and are of the highest importance but are only touched upon in this book. This is because an adequate discussion of how one becomes a Christian and is initiated into Christ's holy church requires a book in itself. Several such books are listed under Additional Resources section. Much discussion in this area is currently taking place in The United Methodist Church, and the worship leader is urged to read one or more of these books.

Not all public worship is dealt with in this book. It deals with the congregation's principal weekly service(s), called the Sunday service because it is usually held on Sunday morning, though sometimes held at other times such as Saturday or Sunday evening. Praise and prayer services of various kinds (prayer and praise, praise and worship, prayer meetings, love feasts, hymn sings) are also important (see *UMH* 876-79; *BOW* 568-84) but are outside the scope of this book. So are evangelistic or seeker services that are targeted primarily to persons outside the congregation, although we shall stress that congregational worship also needs to be evangelistic and sensitive to the needs of seekers. So also are sacred concerts, weddings (*UMH* 864-69; *BOW* 115-38), funerals and memorial services

(*UMH* 870-75; *BOW* 139-71), healing services (*BOW* 613-29), and the many varieties of services for special occasions in the local church and in the wider church (*BOW* 581-612, 630-743).

Finally, the scope of this book is limited to United Methodist congregations in the United States. Much worship of great creativity and vitality is taking place in United Methodist congregations in other countries, but that needs to be the focus of other books.

With this in mind, let us turn to the focus of this book: the Sunday service in United Methodist congregations.

THE CHALLENGE OF FREEDOM

While the resources mentioned above give you basic structure and guidance, they also give you so much freedom that you may find it a bit frightening. The great degree of freedom in worship given to Christians by the Bible is evidenced by the enormous diversity of worship forms and styles among Christians. There is also a wide diversity in the worship that takes place in United Methodist congregations each week.

The United Methodist Church has set very few limits on worship in *The Book of Discipline*,[4] which is our book of church law. It is revised every four years, and in the rest of this book it will be referred to simply as the *Discipline*, followed by the year, paragraph, and page number.

Our hymnal and *Book of Worship* are resources, not books of law. Your congregation is neither required to use the acts and services of worship in these books nor forbidden to use acts and services of worship that you find elsewhere or create for yourselves. How to use this freedom is up to you and your congregation.

Even with so much freedom, it is tempting to take the easy way out and stick with what you are accustomed to doing. If you are an experienced pastor or musician, you can just follow the order of worship and use the hymns and other acts of worship that you already know. If you are new at planning and leading worship, you can recall the worship you have experienced in the past—in your present congregation or in some other congregation—and do your best to duplicate it. You may assume that what you are comfortable with will suit everyone else.

But as you soon discover, this is not necessarily so. What is familiar and comfortable for you is often strange and uncomfortable to other people. The congregation's needs must also be met, as must the needs of those you hope to attract to your congregation. What the pastor wants, what the musical leadership wants, what most of the congregation want, what significant minorities in the congregation want, and what would appeal to the unchurched people who live within range of your congregation's ministries may be many different things. How do you take them all into account as you plan and lead congregational worship?

Many in your congregation may assume that its worship practices are *the* United Methodist way, but in our diverse denomination this simply is not true. A United Methodist who moves into your community may find your worship quite strange. When you go to another community you may find unfamiliar worship practices in the United Methodist congregation(s) there. Some of the varieties of United Methodist worship practice, and some of the reasons for our diversity, will be discussed in this book. Knowing what other United Methodists do can give you and your congregation a wealth of new ideas, some of which you may want to adopt.

If your congregation has a history of more than a few years, you may be sure that its worship has not always been the way it is today. It is not really true that "we've always done it this way." Every worship tradition was once new, and it got started for a reason. Many traditions are not nearly so old as some people think they are. Traditions were often started for reasons that would surprise the people who follow them today.

Worship does change. Where your congregation is now is a waystation on its continuing journey. That is why the history of worship is important. This book will help you understand the background of many of the worship practices you are likely to find in your congregation.

There are many voices in our denomination calling for change in our worship practices. These voices differ widely in what they advocate and often contradict one another. This book will discuss some of these proposals and help you understand them, so that you can decide for yourself which of them you should adopt.

As United Methodists we are free to adapt worship to changing times and differing situations and needs. Each congregation and its worship leaders must decide how its worship could be better, and what steps it should take in that direction.

First, however, worship leaders should deal with some fundamental questions. What does "better" mean in worship? What is worship? What is supposed to be happening when we worship? How is the structure and content of our worship related to our basic Christian beliefs? To what extent can we freely adapt our worship of God to give people what they want, and what are the enduring basics that we dare not compromise?

This book is designed to help you and your congregation in the process of finding your own answers to these questions and bringing new life to your congregation's worship.

GETTING FROM HERE TO THERE

It can be extremely frustrating to compare worship as we wish it to be and worship as we now experience it week after week. This frustration may grow as you learn more about worship, get new ideas, and start setting goals. How can your congregation move from where it is toward the goals you have in mind? The gap may seem too great to cross. How do we get from here to there?

Throughout this book there will be practical suggestions to help you do this, but they will be based on the assumption that there are four essentials if your congregation's worship is to be transformed.

1) *Renewal of worship—and the renewal of your congregation and its members—must come from God.* Neither you nor your congregation can force renewal by following a well packaged program, or by remodeling your sanctuary, or by adopting some supposedly "correct" order or style of worship, or by imitating what some "successful" congregation has done. To be sure, inappropriate forms and styles of worship may be barriers to the workings of the Holy Spirit. New forms and styles of worship at their best can remove barriers—can unclog channels—for the Holy Spirit. But no matter how your congregation may re-form or restyle its worship, there is no substitute for constant and prayerful openness to the unpredictable and often astonishing leadings of the Holy Spirit.

2) *Effective leadership that includes the pastor's leadership is essential.* If you are the pastor, you must take leadership and do it effectively if major changes are to be made in your congregation's worship. If you have any other role in your congregation, you should take the leadership that is possible in your role and help the pastor take the leadership that only a pastor can take. Effective leadership depends on the congregation's trust and must be earned if it is to last beyond a brief initial "honeymoon period."

3) *Effective leadership requires planning and teamwork.* Congregations with vital worship carefully plan their services. This is just as true when the service itself seems informal and spontaneous as it is when the service is more formal. It is essential that the pastor work in close cooperation with those who have musical responsibilities and with any others who have leadership roles in congregational worship. This cooperative planning must begin well in advance and lead to effective teamwork during worship. The *Discipline* (1992, Par. 262.11*a*, p. 158) also gives an important cooperative role in worship planning to the worship chairperson. Other members may be added to form a worship committee, which can be extremely helpful. Detailed suggestions for team planning of worship are found in *Guidelines for Leading Your Church 1993-1996:*

Worship (164540), in *Your Ministry of Planning Worship Each Week* (Discipleship Resources W134K), and in Thomas A. Langford's *Blueprints for Worship* (Abingdon 033128), all of which are available from Cokesbury.

4) *The people must feel at home with their worship.* Effective worship must be in the heart language of the worshipers. People's heart language can grow, but this takes time. Any changes should be interpreted to the people, and they must gain ownership of these changes. When this happens and the present pastor or musical leaders are replaced by others, the people will not say, "That was so-and-so's idea." They will say, "This is the way we like it."

With these practical guidelines in mind, we now turn to the basic question: What is Christian worship?

CHAPTER 2

What Is Christian Worship?

†

WORSHIP IS ENCOUNTER

"Our worship in both its diversity and its unity is an encounter with the living God through the risen Christ in the power of the Holy Spirit" (*BOW* 13). This statement on the opening page of our *Book of Worship* expresses our basic understanding of Christian worship. It is a celebration of the gospel in which God calls anew to us through the risen Christ, and the Holy Spirit within us enables us to hear and respond. The rhythms of call and response bring us to a communion that unites us with God and with one another, renewing us as the Body of Christ for the world.

The gospel that we celebrate is God's good news to us. It includes the whole sweep of God's mighty acts from the beginnings of creation to Christ's coming in final victory and the heavenly banquet. This is sometimes called salvation history. It is also creation history and sanctification history.

1) Basic to this history is creation, not only what happened in the beginning, but also God's continuing new creation in us and in all the universe.

2) Central to this history is what God has done for us in Christ's suffering, death, resurrection, and ascension—what is sometimes called the saving work of Christ or the paschal

(passover) mystery. "Our paschal lamb, Christ, has been sacrificed. Therefore, let us celebrate" (1 Cor. 5:7*b*-8*a*).

3) This history also looks forward. When the Holy Spirit enables us to encounter the living Christ and say with Thomas, "My Lord and my God!" (John 20:28), we anticipate the ultimate vision of God. We pray at Holy Communion that the Holy Spirit will make us "one with Christ, one with each other, and one in ministry to all the world, until Christ comes in final victory and we feast at his heavenly banquet" (*UMH* 10; *BOW* 38); and the communion that follows is a foretaste of that heavenly banquet.

Since we are made one, not only with Christ but also with one another, Christian congregational worship is far more than the worship of a number of solitary individuals. The Holy Spirit enables it to be an encounter of the assembled congregation both with God and with one another in the name and through the presence of Jesus Christ. Those assembled are renewed as the Body of Christ.

Even though in congregational worship God may speak very personally to the depths of my heart and I may silently utter a very personal prayer, I am not alone with God. It is a great support to be surrounded and upheld by other worshipers. Not only the preacher, but also others in the congregation as well may help bring God's Word to me, and when my faith is weak it is strengthened by the faith of those around me.

But there is something even more glorious in our worship. Those people who are visibly assembled around me are by no means the whole worshiping assembly. "With your people on earth and all the company of heaven we praise your name and join their unending hymn" (*UMH* 9; *BOW* 36). "Therefore with angels and archangels, and with all the company of heaven, we laud and magnify thy glorious name" (*UMH* 28; *BOW* 47). These praises at Holy Communion express our conviction that with us as we worship is the living presence of the whole body of Christians of all times and all places. Spiritually with us are Christians around the world today, those who have died and praise God "with all the company of

¶ *17*

heaven," and indeed generations yet unborn who will praise God's name. The visions granted to John of a great multitude in heaven praising God reveal to us that we too are joined and supported by a great invisible multitude (Rev. 4, 5, and 7:9-17).

And there is more. John "heard every creature in heaven and on earth and under the earth and in the sea, and all that is in them, singing" praise to God (Rev. 5:13). "Let everything that breathes praise the LORD" (Ps. 150:6; *UMH* 862).

Worship is not limited to living creatures: "The heavens are telling the glory of God; and the firmament proclaims [God's] handiwork" (Psalm 19; *UMH* 750).

> Praise the Lord, sun and moon,
> praise the Lord, all shining stars!
> Praise the Lord, highest heavens,
> and all waters above the heavens!
> Let them praise the name of the LORD,
> who commanded and they were created.
> (Ps. 148:3-5; *UMH* 861)

Our worship as Christians is part of the universe whose whole history is an act of worship in which the continuing call of the Creator is answered by the continuing response of the creation in a communion of Creator and creation.[5]

WORSHIP IS DRAMA

But this grand vision is not what is in the minds of most of us when we gather for worship. God often seems absent rather than present. We do not feel upheld by a vast invisible company of worshipers. We seem to be a gathering of people talking and singing about God and about ourselves rather than encountering God or joining with anyone outside the room where we are meeting.

Worse yet, we may consciously or unconsciously be leading congregations to experience worship as a performance in which the preacher, other leaders, and the choir are actors and chorus on a stage.[6] The people may have been led to see themselves not as a congregation in a sanctuary but as an audience in an auditorium, watching and listening, ready to criticize the performance after it is complete. They may hear the preacher talk about God and about Jesus, but it may never occur to them that God through Christ is present and taking part in what is happening.

If we think of worship as a drama, it is a far greater drama than that. The stage is not just the chancel or platform, it is the whole sanctuary. The entire congregation are actors. The pastor is both the director and one of the actors—in other words, an actor-director. God is both the audience and the playwright. The script is the Scriptures, and the play is the drama of life.

We can think of a worship service as a rehearsal of life. Like other rehearsals, worship services should not be too cut-and-dried for learning to occur. The pastor as director has studied the Script(ure), interprets it, adapts to the situation in which the drama is taking place (life here and now), and works to bring the actors and the action together into a coherent whole.

But remember, God the Playwright is present and has a right to interpret the script. This playwright doesn't have to sit back passively beyond the footlights but may walk on stage and mingle with the actors. This playwright may whisper to the director, who in turn can relay the word to the other actors; but this playwright is equally free to speak directly to any of the actors. We directors may resent such a meddlesome playwright, but that's the kind of playwright God is.

After this weekly rehearsal the actors scatter, better prepared to perform their various roles on the larger stage of the world in the drama of life all through the week. On this larger stage they are joined by countless other actors and by other directors and would-be directors. And the Playwright is still present.

But if we think of rehearsals as taking place simply for the sake of later performances, worship services are more than rehearsals. In their own right they are crucial parts of the performance of life itself, serving as models for the rest of the performance. As foretastes of the heavenly banquet, they are meant to be life itself as it should be lived. The way in which we relate to God and to other people in worship should be a model for the way in which we do so during the week.

What would happen to your planning and leading of congregational worship if you took this understanding of worship seriously? What would happen in your congregation if even a few persons dared to take it seriously? Do you really believe that the life of your congregation and of every person in it is part of a vast drama and that your part—and every person's part—is important to the Playwright, even though you do not know the whole plot and even though your local congregation is a tiny part of the whole cast? Do you dare to trust and act on this belief? Do you seriously study the Script(ures) for the drama and seek the help of the Playwright and of others who can help you interpret that script? Are you sensitive to the other actors, relating your role to theirs and learning from them? Are you learning so that in the coming week you will play your part well in the rest of the drama of life?

VARIETIES OF GIFTS AND SERVICES

So far we have been thinking mainly of the congregation as a whole as actors in the drama of worship, but different members of the congregation play different roles. Paul tells us in 1 Corinthians 12:4-31 that there are varieties of gifts and varieties of service in the Body of Christ. We have already compared the pastor to an actor-director in the drama of worship.

The persons who lead worship, whether they are clergy or laypersons, have a dual role in the ongoing interaction between God and the congregation. Sometimes they are spokespersons for God to the people, as when reading scripture passages and preaching; and sometimes they are spokespersons for the people to God, as when leading prayer. Today more and more laypersons are assuming leadership roles in worship. This follows ancient Christian custom and has brought new life to many congregations.

What distinctive gifts, then, does the ordained minister bring to worship, and what does ordination authorize a minister to do in worship? Ordination authorizes the minister: (1) to preach the Word (interpret the Scriptures); (2) to officiate at baptisms, the Lord's Supper, weddings, and funerals; and (3) to order the worship of the congregation within the prescribed guidelines. It is a triple ministry of Word, sacrament, and order. In a United Methodist congregation where no ordained minister is available, the bishop may give an unordained pastor temporary and local authorization to carry on these essential ministries in that congregation.

The ordained minister is the authorized representative of the wider church and its heritage in the local congregation at worship, so that this worship may be more fully the worship of the whole communion of saints. The wider church certifies by ordination its confidence that this minister: (1) has been called by God to this particular ministry; (2) has the faith, commitment, and gifts required for this ministry; and (3) has completed the studies and other preparation necessary for this ministry. The church, through a process involving both the congregations out of which candidates come and then the wider denomination (district and annual conference), examines candidates for ordination, certifies that they are called and qualified, and then invokes the Holy Spirit in ordaining them.

Choir directors, choir members, and those who play musical instruments bring special gifts to worship through the ministry of music—their calling and commitment, their talents, their training and education, and their experience. This is true of the ready and willing persons with little or no training who offer the best that they have to give, just as it is true of the professional musicians who offer their best.

What is a choir? Actually, the congregation as a whole acts as the choir in singing hymns, songs, choruses, and responses. They act as a speaking choir in unison and responsive prayers and other acts of worship. This is part of what was meant by the statement above that the congregation are actors in worship.

But a large choir or chorus may have accompanying instrumentalists and also an inner ensemble of unusually able singers with special responsibilities. Most congregations likewise include one or more smaller ensembles (choirs) and instrumentalists to strengthen the worship of the congregation in three basic ways:

1) They can lead the rest of the congregation in worship. They can strengthen and enrich congregational singing. They can help teach the congregation new hymns and other acts of worship. If they are seated where the rest of the congregation can see them, they can cue the others when to stand and sit and can use their body language to be effective examples of attentive worship.

2) They can be spokespersons for the whole congregation to God. Some acts of worship such as anthems require rehearsal for which the congregation as a whole cannot be expected to give the time. These also often demand special abilities and training that most of the congregation do not have. The rest of the congregation can identify with such acts of worship and feel that the choir and instrumentalists are their spokespersons, offering an act of worship on their behalf to God. Some anthems and cantatas help congregations do this by including singing parts for the whole congregation as well as for the soloists or choir.

3) They can be spokespersons for God to the congregation. God speaks powerfully to people through music. Scripture passages are often opened, and Christian witness given, most effectively when set to music of a type that must be sung or played by an individual or choir rather than by the whole congregation.

Many others bring special gifts to worship. Ushers and greeters play crucial roles, especially in the gathering, at the offering, and during communion. Those who provide or arrange flowers, paraments, banners, and other visuals help the people worship with their eyes. In many congregations worship is enriched by gifts of drama, sacred dance, and related arts. We think of the custodian or whoever cleans and prepares the sanctuary for worship, the church secretary or whoever produces the bulletin, the acolytes and those who train them, and all the other persons in the congregation who have some assigned role in worship. We remember those who serve as worship chairpersons and on worship commissions. We add to all these gifts those that come from individuals who have no assigned role but offer special gifts spontaneously. We remember all the past leaders who still influence worship.

This mind-boggling diversity of gifts is not only rewarding but also sometimes hard to accept. Previous pastors and musicians may have shaped a congregation's experience and expectations in ways that frustrate present leaders. The fussy baby, those who are moved to praise the Lord in the most unexpected time and way, the critic who mumbles a complaining commentary during the service, and the monotone who makes more noise than a dozen people singing in tune are present and worshiping in the same service with perfectionists who feel that their worship has been spoiled if the slightest thing goes wrong, the short-fused who shoot a glare or a frown toward anyone who is the slightest bit conspicuous, and those who seize the slightest excuse to chuckle or snicker. There is no way you or I can make the rest of our congregation be who we might wish them to be, but if we add our gifts to theirs something happens by the grace of God that is beyond anything we could have expected.

WORSHIP IS CENTRAL

Worship is central to the church as a whole, to your local congregation, and to your participation as a Christian in the church and the world.

In worship we discover that we *are* the church. We are reminded of who we are and what, by God's grace, we are becoming. As important as it is to ask and plan what your congregation is *doing* as the church, the most basic thing is *being* the church. You can leave out any other part of your congregation's program or processes, important as it may be, and still have a church if you have regular worship. But if you don't have congregational worship, you may have a group or an organization, but you don't have a church.

Christians are an Easter people. When a few men and women who had been shattered and scattered by Jesus' death found themselves face to face with the risen, living Christ, they found faith and meaning for their lives and a message for the world. The risen Christ promised them, "I am with you always" (Matt. 28:20).

The Holy Spirit enabled them to continue experiencing the presence of the living Christ and united them into the church. Once they were not a people, but now they were God's people (1 Pet. 2:10). They were Christ's family, sisters and brothers to Christ and to one another (Matt. 12:46-50). They were the body of the living Christ, who was their head (Eph. 1:22-23).

Today in the power of the Holy Spirit, the same living Christ does for congregations gathered in worship, week after week, what he did for those disciples on the first Easter Day, but with this difference: now we can come joyfully *expecting* an encounter with the risen Christ and focusing our attention on the fact of his presence. Christ bonds us anew to himself and to one another as his people, his family, his body. Christ enables his body to grow, gives to each member of the body the gifts needed in the roles to which he calls that person, and empowers the church corporately for its witness in the world.

It is no wonder that in most congregations more people are present for worship than at any other single event during the week. Even if there are other occasions when as many people are present as attend Sunday worship—an evangelistic service, a Saturday evening service, a Sunday school assembly, a large wedding or funeral, some special service—these are almost always worship services or at least occasions when worship is an important part of what takes place.

Often in worldwide church history, congregations have flourished with only one scheduled activity each week—worship—during which children, youth, and adults of every age were trained and educated, counseled and advised, nurtured and supported, and equipped for what they were to do in the following week. Today many churches of very small membership have an effective ministry with no regular weekly meetings except congregational worship and perhaps a Sunday school that includes worship.

Imagine the church forced to cut back its program to the absolute minimum, as in times of persecution. There have been, and still are, times and places where congregations as we think of them have not been permitted, where they could gather only as families and small groups in secret. When they managed to come together in such circumstances, their chief and often their only corporate activity was worship.

Even in a large congregation with an extensive seven-day-a-week program, corporate worship is central. To be sure, its members often feel more of a sense of belonging to a Sunday school class, an organization, or a small group within the congregation than to the congregation as a whole. But these smaller groups are likely to have times of worship in their meetings. And the main congregational services of worship are the central act by which a large and diverse congregation is, and recognizes itself as, one congregation rather than many.

It is when it is gathered for worship that a congregation is most open to change and growth. Nothing will permeate the whole life of a congregation with the felt presence and power of God as deeply and pervasively as the coming to life of its corporate worship. Spiritual renewal can certainly originate elsewhere in a congregation than in its corporate worship; but renewal in that case will before long either bring new life to the congregational worship or be severely limited, if not stifled, by the continuing deadness of that worship.

Worship is crucial both in attracting church-shopping visitors and in winning unchurched seekers to Christ and the church. Whatever the process by which persons are attracted to your congregation and its ministries, somewhere in this process they will begin experiencing your congregation at worship. First impressions are especially important.

Visitors probably come with important questions on their minds. Is this the kind of church I am looking for? What does it stand for? Is there anything here that meets my needs? Are these people that I'd like to be associated with? Could I become enthusiastic about what this church is doing? What they experience in your congregation's worship will do much to determine how they answer such questions and whether these answers lead to new or renewed Christian commitment.

As Christians we need to be part of a supportive worshiping community if we are to be nurtured and grow in the faith. Even if we are familiar with the gospel message we need to be reminded of it regularly. We need a deeper understanding of the story and teachings of the Bible. We need to participate in public prayer and learn from the example of other Christians how to pray and praise God in any setting, public or private. We need a model of how Christians show love to one another and act out the gospel. By meeting members of the Body of Christ with differing gifts and perspectives we broaden our horizons and become better grounded and more mature Christians.

FIVE BASIC PRINCIPLES OF WORSHIP

Five basic principles follow from our understanding of worship.

1) *God's Word is primary.* It is given to us in the Scriptures, which are our primary source for discerning what is of God and the "script" on which our worship is based. The

proclamation and interpretation of the Scriptures is central to our congregational worship and should over a period of time include a full and balanced coverage of the whole story and teaching of the Bible. Prayer and praise gain added power when words from the Scriptures are used.

2) *Active congregational participation is crucial.* The call of God's Word requires the response of God's people. The congregation's communion with God and with one another is based upon a call-and-response process of sharing. Prayer and praise, therefore, play a major role in congregational worship. The people need to be able to share their joys and sorrows, their needs and concerns. God has given to members of any congregation varieties of gifts (1 Corinthians 12), which they need to share and which others need to receive. The particular gifts of laypersons as well as clergy are needed, not only in acts of worship but also in its planning, leadership, and evaluation.

3) *Spontaneity and order are both important.* Worship should be open to both the planned and the unexpected movings of the Holy Spirit, who can speak not only through the preacher but through anyone present. People feel free to follow the Spirit if they have a basic sense of pattern and structure, within which there is freedom and from which one may occasionally depart. Both rigidity on the one hand and chaos on the other make most people withdraw into their shells. All should be done in love and for mutual upbuilding, "decently and in order" (1 Corinthians 13 and 14).

4) *Worship should be relevant and inclusive.* Because God relates to all of life, so should worship. It should relate to the people's memories, experiences, needs, and hopes. It should include the stranger as well as those already part of the congregation. It should include emotion as well as thought, the body as well as the mind, and each of the senses. It should include children, youth, and adults of all ages and stages of development in such a way that persons at every level of spiritual development can be reached by God's Word and

appropriately respond. It should include men and women of every racial, ethnic, class, and cultural heritage to which the congregation has access as well as persons with every combination of abilities and limitations. All these persons should be enabled to offer their gifts as well as their needs in worship.

5) *Worship is communion.* It is communion between God and the gathered congregation and communion of persons with God and with one another. It moves through call-and-response sharing to climactic times when we have a foretaste of the heavenly banquet and know ourselves to be "one with Christ, one with each other, and one in ministry to all the world" (*BOW* 38; *UMH* 10). While the Spirit can give this gift when we least expect it, Christ gives us a regular opportunity for such a foretaste in Holy Communion. This sacrament should have the major role in congregational worship that it had in New Testament worship.

CHAPTER 3

The Basic Pattern of Worship and Its Origins

✝

THE BASIC PATTERN

The key page in the hymnal is page 2, the Basic Pattern of Worship. The key section of the *Book of Worship* is pages 13-15, the same Basic Pattern with an "Introduction." If you could only read three pages before planning and leading worship, pages 13-15 of the *Book of Worship* are what I would recommend. Here is the Basic Pattern of Worship:

ENTRANCE

The people come together in the Lord's name. There may be greetings, music and song, prayer and praise.

PROCLAMATION AND RESPONSE

The Scriptures are opened to the people through the reading of lessons, preaching, witnessing, music, or other arts and media. Interspersed may be psalms, anthems, and hymns. Responses to God's Word include acts of commitment and faith with offerings of concerns, prayers, gifts, and service for the world and for one another.

THANKSGIVING AND COMMUNION

In services with Communion, the actions of Jesus in the Upper Room are reenacted:

taking the bread and cup,
giving thanks over the bread and cup,
breaking the bread, and
giving the bread and cup.

In services without Communion, thanks are given for God's mighty acts in Jesus Christ.

SENDING FORTH

The people are sent into ministry with the Lord's blessing.

The Introduction (*BOW* 13-14) is also so important that it would be helpful for you to read or review it now before continuing with this book.

The primary message of both the Introduction and the Basic Pattern is "that behind the diversity of United Methodist worship there is a basic unity" (*BOW* 13).

As you visit United Methodist congregations at worship, you are likely to notice their diversity. Our denomination encourages this diversity.

> When the people of God gather, the Spirit is free to move them to worship in diverse ways, according to their needs. We rejoice that congregations of large and small membership, in different regions, in different communities, of different racial and ethnic composition, and with distinctive local traditions can each worship in a style that enables the people to feel at home. (*BOW* 13)

Because the Bible does not give us detailed guidelines for ordering Christian worship, Christians have been free through the centuries to adapt their worship so that people can hear and respond to the gospel in their own heart language. In every culture in which Christianity has become deeply rooted, that local culture and its traditions have influenced its Christian worship. This adaptability has been a great help in enabling Christianity to spread through the world's diverse cultures. But behind our diverse forms and styles of worship we need a basic God-given unity.

> The Spirit is also the source of unity and truth. The teachings of Scripture give our worship a basic pattern that has proved itself over the centuries, that gives The United Methodist Church its sense of identity and links us to the universal Church. This pattern goes back to worship as Jesus and his earliest disciples knew it—services in the synagogue and Jewish family worship around the meal table. It has been fleshed out by the experience and traditions of Christian congregations for two thousand years. (*BOW* 13)

The Basic Pattern of Worship, which is more flexible and inclusive than any particular order of worship could be, expresses this biblical and historic pattern:

> The Basic Pattern of Worship is rooted in Scripture and in our United Methodist heritage and experience. It expresses the biblical, historical, and theological integrity of Christian worship and is the basis of all the General Services of the Church. (*BOW* 13)

The definite article "the" was placed in the title deliberately and after discussion in recognition that this pattern links a congregation's worship with that of other United Methodists and with the universal church of all times and all places. It continually leads us back to the Bible and its message—to unity in Christian truth.

THE BIBLICAL ROOTS OF THE BASIC PATTERN

Jesus was a Jew. So were his earliest disciples. Jewish synagogue worship and worship around the meal table are the twin taproots through which Christian worship is most deeply rooted.

> The Entrance and the Proclamation and Response—often called the Service of the Word or the Preaching Service—are a Christian adaptation of the ancient synagogue service. The Thanksgiving and Communion, commonly called the Lord's Supper or Holy Communion, is a Christian adaptation of Jewish worship at family meal tables.   (*BOW* 13-14)

Also, as we shall see, our worship has roots in the Jewish Temple.

We are not sure just how and when synagogue worship originated, but by the time of Jesus and his disciples the synagogue, along with the home, was where most Jews worshiped. The Temple still stood in Jerusalem; but since most Jews did not live in Jerusalem and could go there only occasionally, if at all, the synagogue where they lived was the center of their community worship.

The term *synagogue* literally means "gathering" or "assembly." It was applied first to the gatherings themselves, which could be held anywhere and led by any man well enough educated in the Scriptures to read and interpret them. Later the buildings built to accommodate them were also called synagogues. In these gatherings, Jews would read from the Scriptures (what we call the Old Testament), teaching and interpreting these scriptures in the light of the situations in which they found themselves. Interspersed were prayers and praises to God, probably including psalms.

Jesus began his public ministry by going around his native region of Galilee preaching, teaching, and healing in synagogues (Matt. 4:23, 9:35, 12:9-14, 13:54; Mark 1:21-27, 1:39, 3:1-6, 6:2; Luke 4:15, 4:31-36, 4:44, 6:6-11, 13:10-17; John 6:59, 18:20). In his hometown of Nazareth, he went to the synagogue on the sabbath day, as was his custom; read Isaiah 61:1-2 from the Scriptures; and then preached to the congregation (Luke 4:16-30).

When Jesus and his disciples left their families to travel together, they became a family. Jesus said, pointing to his disciples, "Here are my mother and my brothers! For whoever does the will of my Father in heaven is my brother and sister and mother" (Matt. 12:49-50; see also Mark 3:34-35 and Luke 8:21).

As Jesus and his disciples traveled together they also ate together. The meal table was the center of Jewish family worship—on annual occasions such as Passover, on the weekly sabbath, and at daily mealtimes. As a family of devout Jews, Jesus and his disciples considered their meals together sacred occasions to be observed with thanksgiving to God.

The Gospels tell that when Jesus fed the five thousand he did four things that marked this as a sacred occasion. He (1) *took* the loaves and fish, (2) *blessed*—said a blessing or gave thanks to God, (3) *broke* the loaves, and (4) *gave* the loaves and fish to the crowds (Matt. 14:19; Mark 6:41; Luke 9:16; John 6:11). They add that he did the same when he fed the four thousand (Matt. 15:36; Mark 8:6-7).

Jesus' supper with his disciples on the night before his death was both the last of these meals and the beginning of a transformed meal that Christians have eaten ever since. It included the actions that were familiar to the disciples: he *took* a loaf of bread and later the cup, *blessed* or gave thanks over each, *broke* the loaf of bread, and *gave* the loaf and later the cup to the disciples. Then Jesus added something new to the sacred family meal they had known. As he gave them the bread he said, "This is my body. . . . Do this in remembrance of me." As he gave them the cup he said, "This is [the new covenant in] my blood . . . . Do this, as often as you drink it, in remembrance of me" (Matt. 26:26-29; Mark 14:22-25; Luke 22:17-20; 1 Cor. 11:23-25).

The word translated *remembrance* has a meaning stronger than what we ordinarily mean by the word "remember." We might better use the word "recall" in the sense of "call back"— "Do this to call me back."

¶ *33*

The location and timing of this supper and Jesus' death the next day at Passover in Jerusalem also linked them to the Jewish Temple in Jerusalem, where thousands of Jews from far and near had gathered at Passover time to have a part in the sacrifice of lambs. Paul, looking back at Jesus' death, wrote: "Our paschal [Passover] lamb, Christ, has been sacrificed. Therefore, let us celebrate the festival . . ." (1 Cor. 5:7*b*-8*a*). Because Christ's self-sacrifice took the place of temple sacrifices, animal sacrifice would have no place in Christian worship. Instead, proclaiming and recalling Christ's sacrificial death (1 Cor. 1:23-24; 11:26) would link Christian worship with temple worship.

In this context the New Testament occasionally speaks of Christians offering sacrifices: "Present your bodies as a living sacrifice, holy and acceptable to God, which is your spiritual worship" (Rom. 12:1). Gifts are "a fragrant offering, a sacrifice acceptable and pleasing to God" (Phil. 4:18). "We have an altar" (Heb. 13:10). "Through [Christ], then, let us continually offer a sacrifice of praise to God" (Heb. 13:15). "Be a holy priesthood, to offer spiritual sacrifices acceptable to God through Jesus Christ" (1 Pet. 2:5). This language is used in Christian worship to this day.

When Jesus was killed his disciples were shattered and scattered; but two days later, on the first Easter, they found themselves face-to-face with the risen, living Christ. They found faith and meaning for their lives and a message for the world. Ever since, Christians have been an Easter people. Luke 24:13-49 describes encounters of the disciples with the risen Christ in a way that suggests a service of worship—a transformed synagogue service and a transformed holy meal. The noted scripture scholar Norman Perrin wrote of Luke 24, "These narratives, especially the Emmaus road narrative, promise the reader that he or she can know Jesus as risen in the Eucharist" (Service of Word and Table).[7]

Two disciples walking from Jerusalem to Emmaus on the first Easter Day were joined by Jesus, whom they did not recognize. They poured out their hearts to him, and then he quoted to them extensively from "Moses and all the prophets" (parts of what Christians call the Old Testament) and "interpreted" these scriptures to them—a term that to Luke's readers would indicate what was done in the synagogue and its Christian equivalent. When they got to Emmaus and began their evening meal, the two disciples still not recognizing Jesus, he did what he had done before at their meals. "He *took* bread, *blessed* and *broke* it, and *gave* it to them. Then their eyes were opened, and they recognized him. . . . He had been made known to them in the breaking of the bread" (Luke 24:30, 35).

Again, later that evening in Jerusalem, he appeared to a larger group of disciples, ate in their presence, and "opened their minds to understand the scriptures" (Luke 24:33-49).

Indeed, Word and Table had been combined earlier in Luke's Gospel when Jesus, before feeding the five thousand, "spoke to them about the kingdom of God" (Luke 9:11).

John's Gospel (chaps. 20–21) tells not only that the risen Christ ate breakfast with his disciples but also that Thomas, when he encountered the risen Christ, said, "My Lord and my God!" In the centuries since then, Christians have experienced encounters with the risen Christ as encounters with God, and worshiped God through encounters with the risen Christ.

We read that Jesus then ascended to heaven, is at the right hand of God, and "fills all in all" (Acts 1:9-11; Eph. 1:20-23). He promised his disciples, "I am with you always" (Matt. 28:20). In other words, just as God is everywhere and can be encountered and worshiped anywhere, so can the risen and ascended Christ.

There are two accounts of the giving of the Holy Spirit. John 20:19-23 tells that it was given to the disciples privately on the first Easter Day, to equip them for ministry. Acts 1:8 records Jesus' words to the disciples: "You will receive power when the Holy Spirit has come upon you"; and in Acts 2 we read of a public giving of the Holy Spirit on the Day of Pentecost seven weeks after the first Easter, to equip them for mission to the world. Christians through the ages have treasured both these accounts. Christian worship ever since then has been, to repeat the phrase quoted above from our *Book of Worship*, an encounter with the living God through the risen Christ in the power of the Holy Spirit.

After the Day of Pentecost, as the disciples went out preaching and teaching in the power of the Holy Spirit, they continued to take part in synagogue worship wherever they went: (Acts 9:2, 20; 13:5, 13-48; 14:1; 17:1-4, 10-12, 17; 18:4, 19, 26; 19:8; 22:19; 24:12; 26:11) and to break bread as a holy meal in their own gatherings (Acts 2:42, 46). First Corinthians 16:2 places the Christian gatherings "on the first day of every week," the day after the Jewish sabbath.

As their preaching and teaching about Jesus in the synagogues gradually led to a break between the Christians and Jewish synagogues, Christians held their own adaptation of the synagogue service when they gathered on the first day of the week (Sunday) for "the breaking of bread." This adapted synagogue service came to be called the *synaxis*—a word that, like synagogue, means "gathering." Today we often refer to this as the Service of the Word. In addition to reading and preaching the Word of God, these Christians would "with gratitude in [their] hearts sing psalms, hymns, and spiritual songs to God" (Col. 3:16).

Christians continued "the breaking of bread" as part of this same weekly service. They also called it "the Lord's supper" (1 Cor. 11:20) or *koinonia* (1 Cor. 10:16)—a word that the King James Bible translated as "communion" and more recent versions have translated as "participation" or "sharing." The use of the word *eucharisteo* (give thanks) in the accounts of Jesus' institution of the Lord's Supper (Matt. 26:27; Mark 14:23; Luke 22:17, 19; 1 Cor. 11:24) led Christians at an early date also to use the term "eucharist" (thanksgiving) for the holy meal he instituted. To this day these four New Testament terms—breaking of bread, Lord's Supper, Holy Communion, and Eucharist—are all used to refer to this sacred act of eating and drinking with the living Christ.

This combination of Christian synagogue and Christian family meal service became the standard Christian Sunday worship service. Such a combined service is described in Acts 20:7-12. This account as well as Luke 24 indicate that it was apparently an accepted pattern by the time Luke wrote. Our hymnal and *Book of Worship* call it the Service of Word and Table. The two major parts of the service are sometimes referred to as the Service of the Word and the Service of the Table.

The service described in Acts 20:7-12 was held at night "on the first day of the week." Since Sunday was an ordinary work day then, Christians with jobs to go to would need to hold their services at night. It was what we would call Saturday night, since by Jewish and New Testament Christian reckoning the day ran from sunset to sunset rather than by the Roman reckoning of from midnight to midnight. Just as the Jewish sabbath, the seventh day of the week (Gen. 2:2-3, Exod. 20:8-11), lasted and still lasts from sunset Friday to sunset Saturday, so the first day of the week lasted from sunset Saturday to sunset Sunday.

Christians soon began to call the first day of the week "the Lord's Day." Revelation 1:10 indicates that this was a familiar term by the end of the first century. This term was especially appropriate, since on this day they encountered their risen Lord in the holy meal they called "the Lord's supper" (1 Cor. 11:20). The Lord's Day is the most basic day in the Christian calendar.

As you interpret the biblical roots of the Basic Pattern of Worship to your congregation, you may use the Emmaus story (Luke 24:13-35) in your preaching and teaching as suggested on page 14 of the *Book of Worship*.

THE BASIC PATTERN THROUGH THE CENTURIES

The Book of Worship very briefly summarizes developments in this Basic Pattern between New Testament times and the time of John Wesley in the eighteenth century:

> Since New Testament times, this Basic Pattern has had a long history of development. At times this pattern has been obscured and corrupted, and at times it has been recovered and renewed. (*BOW* 14)

You may wish to learn more about the history of Christian worship. A good place to begin is with James F. White's *A Brief History of Christian Worship*, listed at the end of this book under Additional Resources. Here we shall simply mention a few highlights of that history that help us understand how worship in American United Methodist congregations came to be as it is today.

Consider Christian Sunday worship a few years after New Testament times. About A.D. 155 Justin Martyr, writing in his *First Apology* to pagans to correct vicious rumors about what Christians did when they gathered for worship, gave in chapter 67 this description of Christian Sunday worship:

> And on the day called Sunday there is a meeting in one place of those who live in cities or the country, and the memoirs of the apostles [that later became the New Testament] or the writings of the prophets [Old Testament] are read as long as time permits. When the reader has finished, the presider in a discourse [sermon] urges and invites [us] to the imitation of these noble things. Then we all stand up and offer prayers. . . . When we have finished the prayer, bread is brought, and wine with water, and the presider similarly sends up prayers and thanksgivings to the best of his ability, and the congregation assents, saying the Amen; the distribution and reception of the consecrated [bread and wine] by each one takes place and they are sent to the absent by deacons.

Several things are noteworthy about this description.

1) Justin Martyr used secular terms like "reader," "presider," and "discourse" that would have been understood by the pagans to whom he was writing. For the same reason he used the Roman term "Sunday" instead of the New Testament terms "the Lord's Day" or "the first day of the week."

2) Since the Christians described here were under persecution and had to meet secretly in homes, it is likely that services were held in haste and that anything nonessential was omitted, especially anything noisy or otherwise likely to attract public notice. This may be why there was no mention of singing "psalms, hymns, and spiritual songs."

3) This may also explain the simplification of the Lord's Supper. When Jesus instituted the Lord's Supper it was part of a full meal. That meal has now disappeared. The bread and wine are now taken, blessed, and given together and constitute the whole meal. This change would have made excellent sense in a hasty secret meeting.

On the other hand, the meal may have been omitted as a reaction to abuses such as overeating and overdrinking by some while others went hungry, as described in 1 Corinthians 11:17-22. Even today, church groups meeting around in one another's homes sometimes find that the serving of refreshments grows until it gets out of hand and an agreement has to be made to limit refreshments to a token food and drink. Whatever the original reason for the change, the Lord's Supper ever since then has generally been simply bread and wine.

4) The service was not bound to the reading of a fixed text and was very flexible in its details. The number of readings could vary. The preacher could adapt the message to the needs of the occasion. The people's prayers were not fixed in content or wording. The presider, who "sends up prayers and thanksgivings to the best of his ability" in praying the blessing over the bread and wine, was likewise not bound to follow a fixed text.

5) With all this flexibility the Basic Pattern is clear, and it is clear what they considered to be the essentials.

The reading of scripture for "as long as time permits" was clearly an essential part of the service, even when haste was a matter of life and death. Practically no one in the congregation possessed a copy of the Scripture, nor knew how to read. The message that immediately followed the readings was based upon what had just been read and was likewise essential.

Congregational prayer was also clearly essential. Prayers offered in the congregation for one another and for their common needs was a life-and-death necessity. So were the presider's "prayers and thanksgivings" over the bread and wine, with the congregation's "amen" making this everyone's prayer.

Receiving the bread and wine weekly in Holy Communion was clearly an essential for which these early Christians would risk their lives. Deacons would likewise risk their lives carrying the consecrated bread and wine to those who were unavoidably absent.

Two basic questions that we must struggle with today as we plan congregational worship are: (1) Where and to what extent should we adapt worship to the expectations, wants, and needs of the congregation and of those outside the congregation whom we wish to attract? (2) When we cannot include everything in worship that we might wish to, or when there is popular resistance to certain acts of worship, what are our priorities? What are the "majors" and what are the "minors"? What is really essential? The basics found in scripture and the example of these early Christians can help us answer these questions.

During the first three centuries, when Christians were a persecuted minority, several other major developments were taking place in congregational worship.

1) While the presider was not bound to follow a fixed text, a few texts have come down to us that give us an idea of the content of the prayers, especially the Great Thanksgiving

(blessing) over the bread and cup. Study of these has been influential in shaping the Great Thanksgivings in the worship books of Christian denominations today.

2) Christians began to celebrate annual observances as well as the weekly Lord's Day, and specially selected scripture readings were coming to be appointed for the major annual observances. This was the beginning of the Christian Year and of a Christian lectionary (table of scripture readings for the days of the Christian Year).

3) Christians were carefully preparing candidates for baptism and then baptizing them in solemn ceremonies. Such baptismal descriptions and texts as have survived from this period have had a major influence on the baptism resources produced by The United Methodist Church and other denominations in recent years.

4) Christians in many places held congregational worship on weekdays as well as on the Lord's Day. A whole different form of daily praise and prayer service was developing as a complement to the Sunday Eucharist. These early Christian daily prayer services have greatly influenced the United Methodist praise and prayer service resources and those of other denominations.

In the fourth century Christianity was transformed from a persecuted minority religion to the official religion of the Roman Empire. This radical change of status soon brought changes in congregational worship as well.

1) Christians could now for the first time erect church buildings. They no longer had to worship in homes. Large buildings, modeled on the public buildings of the Roman Empire, were now built to accommodate Christian worship. Sometimes temples that had been dedicated to other gods— the Parthenon in Athens, for example—were rededicated to Christian worship. These larger buildings were needed to accommodate the much larger number of worshipers who came now that Christianity was the established religion.

2) Christian worship in these new settings developed impressive entrance ceremonies prior to the reading and preaching of scripture. The Introit was a psalm chanted while the clergy were entering, the ancestor of both our opening or processional hymn and of choir introits. Opening prayer was added, which could include a response such as *Kyrie Eleison* ("Lord, Have Mercy"). Prayers and responses were commonly chanted. The *Kyrie Eleison* in time was also sung as a freestanding acclamation (see *UMH* 482-485). Songs of praise such as the *Gloria in Excelsis* ("Canticle of God's Glory," *UMH* 482-485 and 82-83) became the ancestors of praise songs and anthems that Christians have been writing and using ever since.

These acts of praise and prayer preceding the reading and preaching of scripture were the ancestor of the part of our worship today known as the entrance, also known in some congregations as the praise service or song service. In these ceremonies we can see both the influence of imperial court ceremonies already familiar to the people and the appropriation of elements from Jewish temple worship such as the use of psalms. This was not surprising now that the imperial court was officially Christian and now that the Christians had temples of their own.

3) Worship increasingly followed fixed texts, and a number of such fixed rites developed in different regions. The immense growth in the numbers of Christians and of their clergy, many of whom were inadequately grounded in the faith, increased the risks of freedom in worship. Church councils beginning in the fourth century set the limits of orthodox doctrine and condemned heresies. Fixed worship texts, as well as a closed scriptural canon, were both a guarantee of orthodoxy and a necessity for the many clergy who would have been unable to compose adequate prayers on their own.

During the thousand years that followed, Christian worship in different parts of the world developed in different ways, but what concerns us here are several significant changes that took place in western Europe.

1) The Roman rite gradually replaced other regional liturgies to become dominant in western Europe.

2) The Latin language of the Roman rite ceased to be the language of the people. Partly this was because languages such as French and Italian were evolving out of Latin, and partly it was because Christianity had spread to areas of northern Europe where the people had never spoken Latin. Preaching was in the language of the people but was for the most part not emphasized. The standardized Latin texts made the content of worship easier to control and facilitated the development of liturgical music, but the effect was to reduce the role of the people in worship and the effectiveness of the Word in nurturing faith.

3) Christian piety in general, and the Eucharist in particular, became increasingly centered on the sacrificial suffering and death of Christ rather than on Christ's victorious passage through suffering and death to resurrection. The crucifix, with the figure of a suffering Christ attached to the cross, became a major symbol in worship.

4) The Eucharist itself was commonly called the Mass and came to be understood primarily as a sacrifice. The Lord's table became an altar where the consecrated bread and wine—understood in increasingly literal terms as the body and blood of Christ—were offered to God. The altar came to be placed against the wall, where the priest (the ordained presider, not the whole priestly people), offered the sacrifice with his back to the people. The area where the clergy functioned came to be a separate space called the chancel, increasingly removed from the space called the nave where the people were gathered. Although the Eucharist was celebrated regularly, most people rarely received communion, so that finally they had to be required to receive it at least once a year at Easter. By the fourteenth century only priests were permitted to drink from the cup; and laypersons could receive only the bread, which had become a wafer rather than real bread. Worship became increasingly a spectacle that the people observed from a distance.

The Protestant Reformation in the sixteenth century attempted to reform these abuses.[8] Emphasizing the authority of the Scripture and the need to teach the story and message of the Bible to the people, Protestant churches reformed and strengthened what we call the Service of the Word. They conducted worship in the language of the people; emphasized the reading and preaching of the scriptures; and promoted congregational singing of "psalms, hymns, and spiritual songs." These reforms were greatly facilitated by the invention of printing in the previous century and the relative ease with which books could now be produced and distributed. Some Protestants also restored the freedom to pray extemporaneously rather than being limited to set prayer texts.

They also reformed the understanding and celebration of the Lord's Supper. Emphasizing the once and for all "full, perfect, and sufficient" sacrifice of Christ on the cross for the sins of the world, they denied that in the Lord's Supper the bread and wine were changed in substance into the body and blood of Christ and his body and blood offered again as a sacrifice. Instead, they sought to limit the ideas of Christ's real presence and of sacrifice to what was taught in the New Testament, although they differed among themselves as to exactly what the New Testament taught. Emphasizing the corporate priesthood of the whole people of God, they restored the right of laypersons to drink from the cup as well as eat the bread and also restored the expectation that those present should partake unless there was some reason why they should not.

But the success of the Reformation was only partial. The Roman Catholic Church rejected the Protestant reforms and retained the allegiance of most Christians in western Europe. The Eastern Orthodox and other ancient Eastern churches, which had long since become separated from the Roman Catholic Church, were untouched. Protestants themselves were unable fully to rid themselves of medieval ideas that blocked full renewal.

Protestant piety in general, and understanding of the Lord's Supper in particular, continued as in medieval times to center on Christ's death for the sins of the world. Little was said at the Lord's Supper about God's other mighty acts.

Also, Lord's Supper services came to focus heavily on our human unworthiness and on confession and forgiveness of sin. When Protestants abolished the sacrament of penance with its confession of sins, they could not abolish the human needs to which penance had ministered, and these needs attached themselves to the Lord's Supper.

These emphases tended to make the Lord's Supper solemn, penitential, even funereal. This is reflected, for example, in the Lord's Supper text of the Church of England, which American Methodists inherited. Such emphases are sometimes appropriate, to be sure, and they are a part of the gospel. But they are far from being the whole gospel, and such a Lord's Supper every Sunday would be hard to take.

Given these emphases, and given the fact that the people were conditioned by centuries of having received communion only occasionally, it is not surprising that there was resistance to celebrating the Lord's Supper every Lord's Day, especially since most of the congregation would be expected to receive communion whenever it was celebrated. Some Protestant reformers, including Martin Luther and John Calvin, believed that the Lord's Supper was the natural and appropriate act to follow the weekly Service of the Word. Calvin left record of his deep disappointment because he was unable to persuade the people of Geneva to adopt this practice. Some Protestant congregations followed the advice of these reformers and celebrated the Lord's Supper every Lord's Day, but in the generations that followed the Reformation popular resistance caused this practice to become increasingly rare. Other Reformation leaders were content with a Service of the Word every Sunday, to which the Lord's Supper was added only monthly or quarterly; and this practice generally prevailed.

CHAPTER 4

The Basic Pattern as a United Methodist Heritage

✝

THE WESLEYS

In the centuries since the Reformation, there have been numerous renewal movements in Protestantism that have given new vitality to worship. The United Methodist Church is directly descended from three of these movements that began in eighteenth-century England and America.

In England, John Wesley (1703–1791) was a priest of the Church of England who spent his life leading the renewal movement that became Methodism. His preaching was especially effective with those who were estranged from the church, and he organized them into regularly meeting bands, classes, and societies for their ongoing spiritual nurture. He took care to see that these meetings did not conflict with Sunday services in the local Anglican church and urged his followers to attend worship and receive communion there. His brother Charles (1707–1788), also an Anglican priest, wrote many hymns rich with biblical imagery and teachings, which were then set to familiar tunes that the people could readily sing.

Worship in the Church of England used the texts found in the 1662 revision of *The Book of Common Prayer*, which included among its services daily Morning Prayer and Evening Prayer, the Great Litany (a long intercessory prayer), and the Lord's Supper (both Word and Table, to be celebrated at least on Sundays and holy days). If the prayerbook pattern were fully followed, Sunday worship would begin, as on weekdays, with Morning Prayer. It would then continue with the Great Litany and the Lord's Supper. In practice, however, the Lord's Supper in most congregations by Wesley's time was celebrated only three or four times a year. On other Sundays, Morning Prayer and the Great Litany would be followed by Antecommunion (the first half of the Lord's Supper that we now call the Service of the Word).

John Wesley was unusual among eighteenth-century Anglicans in that he strongly affirmed the prayerbook ideal of the Lord's Supper every Lord's Day. He received communion on an average of twice a week throughout his adult life and declared in his sermon "The Duty of Constant Communion"[9] that "it is the duty of every Christian to receive the Lord's Supper as often as he can." He goes on to make it clear that the Lord's Supper to him is not only a duty but a joy. When this sermon was published in 1787, shortly before his death, Wesley wrote in his introduction "To the Reader": "The following discourse was written above five and fifty years ago. . . . But I thank God I have not yet seen cause to alter my sentiments in any point which is therein delivered." [10] This sermon represents Wesley's fullest and most explicit statement of his eucharistic doctrine and practice.

His brother Charles's beliefs and practice were similar. Charles's 166 "Hymns on the Lord's Supper," some perhaps written or at least edited by John, are an incredibly rich treasury of eucharistic doctrine.[11] The eucharistic teachings of the Wesleys, grounded in the Scripture, form a doctrinal standard to which the eucharistic resources in the hymnal and *The Book of Worship* have earnestly sought to be faithful.

For the Wesleys, there was no conflict between the sacramental and the evangelical. They would have strongly rejected any idea that these two are like the ends of a seesaw, where as one goes up the other goes down. Rather, the preaching of the Word is strengthened and completed by the celebration at the Table. Indeed, John Wesley repeatedly found in his evangelistic ministry that the Lord's Supper was "a converting ordinance" as well as a "means of grace." One of the benefits of the Wesleyan revival to the Church of England was a marked improvement in popular enthusiasm for the Lord's Supper. Rattenbury writes:

> The early Methodists flocked to the celebration of Holy Communion in such numbers that the clergy were really embarrassed with the multitude of communicants with which they had to deal.[12]

BEGINNINGS IN AMERICA

Methodism came to America in the 1760s and was organized into the Methodist Episcopal Church in 1784 under the leadership of Francis Asbury (1745–1816). The American Revolution had made Americans unwilling to take orders in church or state from England. It had also become plain that the American Anglicans, who were soon to organize what is now the Episcopal Church, would not accept the Methodists. Thus the American Methodists became not a movement but a church that had to provide for its own Sunday services, and the same thing happened in England shortly after John Wesley's death.

John Wesley, although he had opposed the American Revolution, bowed to the inevitable and recognized the need of the American Methodists for guidance in their worship. He prepared for them an abridged and revised version of *The Book of Common Prayer*, which he called *The Sunday Service of the Methodists in North America*.[13] This book included among its services complete texts for Morning Prayer, Evening Prayer, the Litany, and the Lord's Supper. In the preface to the book he wrote:

I believe there is no Liturgy in the World, either in ancient or modern language, which breathes more of a solid, scriptural, rational Piety, than the Common Prayer of the Church of England. . . . Little alteration is made in the following edition of it (which I recommend to our Societies in North America) except in the following instances: . . . 2. The Service of the Lord's Day, the length of which has been often complained of, is considerably shortened.[14]

In the letter to the North American Methodists that accompanied his book, Wesley wrote: "I also advise the elders to administer the supper of the Lord on every Lord's day."[15]

On the other hand, in the same letter he wrote:

As our American brethren are now totally disentangled both from the State, and from the English Hierarchy, we dare not intangle [*sic*] them again, either with the one or the other. They are now at full liberty, simply to follow the scriptures and the primitive church. And we judge it best that they should stand fast in that liberty, wherewith God has so strangely made them free.[16]

Methodists and United Methodists have struggled with the implications of this mixed message ever since.

In 1792, the Methodist Episcopal Church officially abandoned most of Wesley's *Sunday Service* book, including the texts for Morning and Evening Prayer, the Litany, and the first part of the Lord's Supper (what we call the Service of the Word). In their place these directions "for uniformity in public worship among us, on the Lord's day," were placed in the book of church law known as the *Discipline:* "Let the morning-service consist of singing, prayer, the reading of one chapter out of the Old Testament, and another out of the New, and preaching." Similar directions were given for afternoon and evening services.[17]

The text for the latter part of the Lord's Supper (what we call the Service of the Table) was retained.[18] This left American Methodists with a flexible, oral Sunday service, well-suited to conditions on the frontier, rather than a fixed text, except when the Lord's Supper texts were added following a preaching service.

Radical as these changes were, they respected the priorities that we saw in the worship of the persecuted early Christians and that we see in the Basic Pattern of Worship today. The reading of a generous quantity of scripture is to be followed by biblical preaching. Before, and possibly interspersed with, the proclamation of the Word there is to be praise and prayer. This is clearly a Service of the Word. The retention of full texts for the Service of the Table shows respect for eucharistic doctrine and practice, which would very likely be distorted or lost if left to be improvised by frontier preachers.

The Lord's Supper came to be celebrated monthly or quarterly rather than every Lord's Day, for a combination of reasons whose relative importance scholars still debate. (1) Presiding at the Lord's Supper, unlike preaching, was restricted to the few ordained elders. Most Methodists could receive communion only occasionally, such as when the presiding elder (now called district superintendent) held quarterly conference. (2) Methodists were influenced by customs of monthly or quarterly communion in other denominations and by prevailing enlightenment rationalism that considered the sacraments much less important than preaching. (3) Requiring that a prayerbook-style text be read as the Lord's Supper ritual made it less popular among Methodists because it was uncongenial to their oral culture and a jarring change of style from their preaching services. This was particularly true when, to keep the service from being too long, preaching and other familiar acts of worship were shortened or omitted. (4) The heavily penitential texts, particularly when combined with warnings against receiving communion unworthily, would have been oppressive every Sunday and were more suited to an occasional service of penitence and renewal.

Meanwhile, several men who were kindred spirits to Wesley and Asbury were preaching spiritual renewal among German-speaking Americans. Jacob Albright (1759–1808), originally a Lutheran and also associated for a time with the Methodists, founded the Evangelical Association. Philip Otterbein (1726–1813) and Martin Boehm (1725–1812) led in the formation of the United Brethren in Christ, whose organization was completed under the leadership of Christian Newcomer (1749–1830). Otterbein was a Reformed pastor, while Boehm's and Newcomer's heritage was Mennonite.

What separated them from the Methodists at that time was not doctrine or forms of worship but their call to minister in the German language rather than in English. They shared with the Methodists a passion to bring Christ to persons who were not being reached by existing churches and a devotion to scriptural preaching and to the sacraments. In the journal of Christian Newcomer from 1796 through 1829, for instance, he records 205 "sacramental meetings," which were his chief and most fruitful method of evangelism, as well as 15 other celebrations of the Lord's Supper.[19] Evangelicals and United Brethren settled into a pattern of preaching services similar to those of the Methodists, with the Lord's Supper added monthly or quarterly.

African Americans formed a substantial part of American Methodism from its beginnings. Not only did they worship in the spirit of their African American heritage, they significantly influenced all Methodist worship and have continued doing so to this day. If we ask why early Methodist worship in America was so different from the Methodism in Britain that Wesley knew, and if we wonder at the vigor and fervor of its praise, prayer, and preaching, much of this was due to the fact that the American Methodist heritage reached back to Africa as well as Europe. The strong and clear call-and-response character of African American worship influenced many European American Methodists and has helped us to see the call-and-response character of all Christian worship. Celebrations of the Lord's Supper in African American congregations through the years have tended to be more frequent and better attended than in European American congregations.[20]

During the nineteenth and twentieth centuries the pattern of Sunday worship in Methodist, Evangelical, and United Brethren congregations went through several stages.

THE AGE OF PREACHING POINTS AND MEETINGHOUSES

The first stage, from the late-eighteenth to the mid-nineteenth century, was one of rapid growth. Sunday services of singing, free prayer, scripture reading, and biblical preaching seemed to fit the needs of the American people very well. Methodists so shaped, and were shaped by, the American culture that they became, in their own eyes and often in the eyes of others, the most American of denominations. Evangelicals and United Brethren began making the transition from the German to the English language and assimilating to the Anglo-American culture, while Methodists began ministering to peoples who used languages other than English. By 1850 three out of every eight church members in the United States and 5 per cent of the total population belonged to a predecessor denomination of The United Methodist Church.

At first most congregations worshiped in private homes, secular buildings, or out of doors; and as they began to build their own buildings these were simple meetinghouses. Wesley's words to the British Methodists were incorporated into all the early American Methodist Disciplines:

> Let all our Chapels be built plain and decent; but not more expensively than is absolutely unavoidable: Otherwise the necessity of raising Money will make Rich Men necessary to us. But if so, we must be dependent on them, yea, and be governed by them. And then farewell to Methodist Discipline, if not Doctrine too.[21]

THE AGE OF PULPIT AND PLATFORM

The second stage, from the middle of the nineteenth century until the early-twentieth century, was a time of slower growth—growth that kept the denominations that are now United Methodist at about 5 per cent of the American population but fell behind the growth of organized religion as a whole. Their success in the early years and their continually increasing affluence had become a mixed blessing. As industrialization, immigration, urbanization, and growing sophistication were changing America, they tended to be self-satisfied with their success and ambivalent about adapting to these changes. In Sunday worship and architecture for worship, as in other matters, Methodists, Evangelicals, and United Brethren were divided over whether and how to change with the times.

Some congregations during the nineteenth century, especially its latter half, became affluent and adopted more elaborate forms of worship. They built increasingly impressive buildings with increasingly ornate sanctuaries for worship and were probably relieved when Wesley's words about church building were first softened and then removed from the *Discipline*. They added choirs, organs, and trained musicians and fleshed out the Basic Pattern of Worship with more sophisticated hymns and anthems, recitations of the Lord's Prayer and the Apostles' Creed, sung responses such as the doxology and the Gloria Patri, and responsive readings. They took congregational literacy for granted and increasingly read their acts of worship from a printed page. Late in the century, a few churches contracted with printers for service bulletins on special occasions or even every Sunday. The "amens" and other spontaneous responses that had been commonplace in earlier days were increasingly frowned upon and in more and more congregations entirely disappeared. In successive Methodist *Disciplines* during the century the directions for Sunday services, which by the end of the century had become an outlined order of worship, followed the lead of these congregations.

Some Methodist leaders were even attracted by the Order for Morning Prayer in Wesley's *Sunday Service*.[22] They noticed that Wesley had urged its use every Lord's Day, though they were strangely silent about the fact that Wesley had also advised ordained elders to administer the Lord's Supper every Lord's Day. These leaders may have been influenced by American Episcopal churches, whose prevailing pattern of worship on most Sundays had become Morning Prayer and Sermon—a pattern that had begun to appear in the Church of England during Wesley's lifetime and which he deplored. In any event, the orders of worship in Methodist *Disciplines,* and ultimately in *The Methodist Hymnal* (1905) began to show the influence of the Anglican Morning-Prayer-and-Sermon pattern. Beginning with *The Methodist Hymnal* (1878) there were also fewer and fewer Wesley hymns and more and more Anglican hymns such as "Holy, Holy, Holy."

A great many Methodists resisted these developments. Numerous congregations continued in the old ways or adapted their services in different ways, such as opting for a revivalistic pattern where the sermon was preceded by a song service featuring gospel songs and choruses based on popular musical styles. In congregations where services were becoming more elaborate and formal, many persons found such worship unsatisfying and worshiped less formally but with more satisfaction in Sunday school, Sunday evening services, midweek services, and revival meetings. In many churches there was a large body of adults as well as children and youth who went home after Sunday school; they had had their worship and did not need to attend the preacher's service.

These developments caused controversies that often pitted pastors against musicians, and either or both of these leaders against many in their congregations. Resulting compromises often produced Sunday services about which everyone had mixed feelings and no one was enthusiastic. Nostalgia was often expressed for the "good old days" of early Methodism, though there was much ignorance and confusion about what those "good old days" were really like.

Both factions shared a preference for a sanctuary with a raised platform with a central pulpit on it, symbolizing the centrality of the reading and preaching of God's Word. The communion table was usually in front of the pulpit on a lower level. There might be a baptismal font to one side on the lower level. The choir usually sat in a loft behind the pulpit or to one side of the pulpit, facing the congregation. The sanctuary was often wide, with curved (sometimes almost semicircular) seating, frequently with a balcony, so as to bring the people as close as possible to the pulpit and choir. There was usually no center aisle, so that the preacher looking straight ahead would see people rather than an empty aisle. Many such pulpit-centered sanctuaries are still in use today.

Ironically, this pulpit-centered design did not prevent both opposing factions from sharing in an ominous trend—a gradual decline in the amount of scripture read and in the biblical content of preaching. *The Methodist Episcopal Discipline* (1864) and the *Methodist Episcopal South Discipine* (1866) changed the direction that a chapter from the Old Testament and a chapter from the New Testament be read before preaching to a direction that a lesson (length unspecified) from each Testament be read. This probably reflected what was already common practice. Preaching during this period had come commonly to be based on a text consisting of a single verse or even part of a verse of scripture. Indeed, the text was sometimes a pretext for a sermon that did not interpret the meaning of the text at all but used a key word or phrase or image to launch into an unrelated topic that appealed to the preacher.

The following common Order of Public Worship, agreed upon by both the Methodist Episcopal and Methodist Episcopal South Churches and printed facing the title page of *The Methodist Hymnal* (1905), reflected a continuation of these developments and a desire to please the diverse factions by indicating with brackets parts that may be omitted:

[I.   VOLUNTARY, instrumental or vocal.]
II.   SINGING FROM THE COMMON HYMNAL.
[III.   THE APOSTLES' CREED] (text printed in full)

IV.   PRAYER, concluding with the Lord's Prayer.

[V.   ANTHEM OR VOLUNTARY.]

VI.   LESSON FROM THE OLD TESTAMENT, which, if from the Psalms, may be read responsively.

[VII.   THE GLORIA PATRI.] (text and music printed in full)

VIII.   LESSON FROM THE NEW TESTAMENT.

IX.   NOTICES, FOLLOWED BY COLLECTION; during or after which an offertory may be rendered.

X.   SINGING FROM THE COMMON HYMNAL

XI.   THE SERMON.

XII.   PRAYER. (XII and XIII may be reversed.)

XIII.   SINGING FROM THE COMMON HYMNAL.

XIV.   DOXOLOGY AND THE APOSTOLIC BENEDICTION (2 Cor. 13:14).

This order is especially significant because it was generally used for the next generation and is used with minor variations in some congregations to this day.

This order reflected the continuing diminishment of scripture. While the placement of the Psalter in the back of the 1905 *Hymnal* was a gain, the permission to substitute a psalm for the Old Testament lesson had the effect that many congregations rarely heard readings from the other thirty-eight books of the Old Testament. The insertion of notices (announcements), collection, offertory music, and a hymn between scripture reading and sermon both reflected and encouraged the increasing likelihood that the preaching would not be closely related to the scripture lesson.

THE AGE OF ALTAR AND CHANCEL

The third stage was the "high church" or aesthetic or romantic movement in worship that developed in the Church of England and the Episcopal Church in America in the nineteenth century and became increasingly popular in American Protestant churches in the early- and middle-twentieth century. In some ways this was a continuation of trends already described above, but these were now carried much further. As church people became increasingly sophisticated during and after the 1920s, they became more demanding in their aesthetic taste. As America became more secular during this period, the desire of congregations to retain their members became dominant over their desire to gain converts. As players of any game know, a desire not to lose is quite different from a desire to win and tends to lead to quite different tactics.

Many thought that if services were more beautiful and impressive, people who had outgrown simpler expressions of religion would continue to find worship meaningful. They wanted to enrich worship with beautiful liturgies, music, and other arts such as stained glass. In the prosperous 1920s and the even wider prosperity after World War II, many congregations were able to act on these wishes.

This movement romanticized the Middle Ages as "the age of faith" and the great medieval cathedrals as supreme expressions of faith. Many larger church buildings had already been built to look more or less medieval in the late–nineteenth and early–twentieth centuries. By the 1920s some splendid Neo-Gothic churches were being built, and increasingly their sanctuaries had what were called *divided chancels.* When Gothic architecture became too expensive, especially after World War II, buildings of less expensive architecture such as Georgian (colonial) would be built with divided chancels, and older sanctuaries would be remodeled with them.

Such sanctuaries were divided into two distinct worship spaces, more or less imitating medieval worship spaces. The raised area up front, known as the *chancel,* was likely to be a large, recessed area—almost a separate room—behind an archway. Sometimes a compromise was made, especially if an older sanctuary was being remodeled, and the chancel was simply a platform. Against the center of the far chancel wall was a table, altar, or shelf intended to be the center of worship.

Some persons preferred to reserve the term *sanctuary* for the space immediately around the altar. A cross and candles on the altar symbolized the presence of God. The pulpit was on one side of the chancel, and on the other side there was usually a lectern. The chancel was occupied not only by clergy and other worship leaders but also by the choir, which usually sat at right angles to the people, often in two banks on either side of the altar.

The rest of the people sat in the other distinct area, called the *nave*. It was on a level lower than the chancel and was likely to be long and narrow, with the people usually sitting in straight rows facing the chancel and altar. There was now a center aisle, which made choir, clergy, and wedding processions highly visible and presented no problem when preaching was from a side pulpit.

Sometimes part of the congregation sat in side areas toward the front, called *transepts*, which together with the nave and chancel gave the church a cross-shaped floor plan. Seating in the transepts was at right angles to that in the nave, so that the people there also faced the chancel and altar. Throughout services, the people were encouraged to focus their attention on the altar rather than on the preacher, the choir, or the rest of the congregation.

Such an environment for worship, while it was often created chiefly for reasons of fashion or aesthetics, both reflected and encouraged a more formal style of worship. If all people saw of one another during worship was the backs of the heads of those in front, it was easy to feel alone with God rather than among God's celebrating people. Focusing people's attention on an altar against the far wall suggested that God was "out there" somewhere rather than in the midst of the people. This suggestion was accentuated if the pastor prayed and the choir sang facing the altar, with their sides or backs to the rest of the people.

Centering worship on what was commonly called an altar and commonly looked more like an altar of sacrifice than like a table went along with a theology that regarded worship primarily as an offering to God. In response to what God has done, we offer our praise, our gifts, and ourselves as a spiritual sacrifice to God.

Such God-centered worship was commended as being "objective," in contrast to "subjective" worship that was concerned with evoking inward responses in the worshipers. Instead of asking, "What am I getting out of this service?" one should ask, "What am I putting into this service?" Kierkegaard's saying that the congregation are the actors and God is the audience was often quoted.[23] It was natural to conclude that "only the best" should be offered to God—the most elegant liturgical language, the highest quality of music and other arts, generous gifts of money, and a congregation offering themselves dressed in their Sunday best.

Choir and clergy vestments fit naturally into this style of worship. A few Methodist choirs had begun to vest as early as the 1890s, and by the mid-twentieth century one could expect to find vested choirs in medium-sized and larger congregations. Black clergy robes were already appearing in Methodist services in the 1920s and became commonplace by the 1950s. By the 1950s and 60s a stole in the seasonal color might be worn over the robe, and the robe itself might be white in the summer.

An adaptation of Anglican Morning Prayer and Sermon seemed a fitting order of worship understood as offering. Here is Order of Worship I, which preceded the title page of the 1939 edition of *The Methodist Hymnal* (1935), compared with Wesley's Order for Morning Prayer, taken from the Church of England:

1939 Methodist	Wesley's Morning Prayer
THE PRELUDE.	
THE CALL TO WORSHIP.	SENTENCES OF SCRIPTURE
A HYMN.	
THE PRAYER OF CONFESSION.	THE GENERAL CONFESSION
THE SILENT MEDITATION.	

THE WORDS OF ASSURANCE.   THE PRAYER FOR PARDON

THE LORD'S PRAYER.   THE LORD'S PRAYER

THE ANTHEM OR CHANT.   THE GLORIA PATRI

  Which may be the *Venite*   (Wesley had removed the

  or the *Te Deum.*   *Venite* from Morning Prayer.)

THE RESPONSIVE READING.   PSALM (S)

THE GLORIA PATRI.   THE GLORIA PATRI

THE AFFIRMATION OF FAITH.   OLD TESTAMENT LESSON

THE LESSON FROM THE HOLY   THE *TE DEUM*

  SCRIPTURES.   NEW TESTAMENT LESSON

    PSALM 100

    THE APOSTLES' CREED

THE PASTORAL PRAYER.   PRAYERS

THE OFFERTORY.

A HYMN.

THE SERMON.

THE PRAYER.

THE INVITATION TO CHRISTIAN DISCIPLESHIP.

A HYMN OR DOXOLOGY.

THE BENEDICTION.   BLESSING

THE SILENT PRAYER.

THE POSTLUDE.

If one takes Morning Prayer and adds hymns and organ music and then adds offering and sermon after the closing prayers, as in Morning Prayer and Sermon, the result is very much like the 1939 Methodist order, which was often called Morning Worship. *The Book of Worship* (1945), *The Book of Worship* (1965), and *The Methodist Hymnal* (1966) retained essentially the same order of worship. The 1965 and 1966 books even moved the Affirmation of Faith so that it followed the scripture readings, as in Anglican Morning Prayer. There was no official provision for announcements, but in practice they were commonly made immediately before the Offertory. Meanwhile *The Hymnal* (1957) of the Evangelical United Brethren Church contained a similar order of worship.

Note that whereas in the 1905 order of worship the term *offertory* referred to music offered during or after the *collection*, it was now the term for the offering of money gifts and the increasingly elaborate ceremony that surrounded it. Typically the ushers came forward, the pastor offered a prayer, the ushers received empty offering plates from the pastor and passed them throughout the congregation, and the congregation sang an act of praise or dedication as the filled plates were carried forward and placed as an offering on the altar— all this in addition to whatever other music was sung or played during or after the offering. This ceremony was interpreted as not only the offering of gifts to the church but also a symbolic offering of ourselves and all that we have to God. There could hardly be a clearer example of worship as our offering something on an altar to God.

This interpretation was in some tension not only with previous ideas about the "collection" but also with the placement of the offering during what seemed to many like an intermission in the service. In some congregations the offering was moved to be a response after the sermon and interpreted as the dedicatory climax to the service, a move that often encountered intense resistance.

This order of worship, particularly the placement of confession in it, was frequently defended by reference to Isaiah 6:1-8, although Isaiah's account of his call from God is not a description of congregational worship and could be countered by other scripture passages that suggest different orders—Psalms 19 and 51, for example. Although Isaiah 6:1-8 is not specifically mentioned in *The Book of Worship* (1945), this order of worship was interpreted there as following a fourfold pattern: the adoration of God, the confession of sin, the affirmation of faith, and the dedication of life. These are "attitudes of the devout worshiper presented in ascending movements." "They imply the divinely descending movements of vision, pardon, illumination, and fruition";[24] but the emphasis is clearly on worship as our offering to God.

Reading of scripture in worship seems to have reached a low point during this period, but there was a growing movement to read more scripture. In practice many congregations had no scripture reading at all in worship, and actually including the readings provided for in the official orders of worship would have represented an improvement. In the 1939 order there was a single "Lesson from the Holy Scriptures," in addition to the responsive reading. In *The Book of Worship* (1945) there were "The Lessons from the Old and New Testament Scriptures" as well as the responsive reading. In *The Book of Worship* (1965) and *The Methodist Hymnal* (1966) appears the rubric: "Here shall be read two lessons, one from the Old Testament and one from the Epistles or Gospels." *The Hymnal* (1957) of the Evangelical United Brethren Church suggested two lessons and a responsive reading from the scriptures and further suggested that the Old Testament, Epistles, and Gospels all be represented in these three readings.

Sunday morning worship was now sharply divided into two parts, separated by a sort of intermission. A formal praise and prayer service ending with the pastoral prayer was followed by announcements, offertory, and hymn, which in turn were followed by the sermon and closing acts of worship. This division of the service was emphasized in churches with divided chancels when the service before the offertory was conducted from the lectern, the offertory was conducted from the altar, and the sermon was preached from the pulpit.

The reading and preaching of scripture were widely separated, in space as well as time if one walked away from the Bible on the lectern to preach in the pulpit, making it hard to preach on more than a verse or phrase of "text" that might be quoted immediately before or during the sermon.

Furthermore, the prevailing concept of worship as something we offered to God could be more easily made to fit the first part of the service than the sermon. Some people even made a distinction between the "worship" (the first part of the service) and the sermon.

The two parts of the service seemed to be in a win-lose competition that made them seem like the ends of a seesaw—

when one went up the other went down. Some pastors elaborated and extended the "worship" past the halfway point in the service and shortened their sermons, provoking cries of "high church" and "the slow murder of the sermon." Others preached long sermons, reduced the first part of the service to "preliminaries," and were considered "low church."

Such controversies made it evident that there was still widespread resistance to the form and style of worship that was in fashion. The official hymnals and books of worship during this period all included alternative orders of worship that were somewhere between the 1905 order and the more elaborate orders based on Morning Prayer and Sermon. Some congregations continued in the revivalistic pattern of song service followed by preaching. Some congregations refused to use the official hymnals and instead used commercial hymnals featuring gospel songs and choruses. The denominational publishing houses found it advisable to publish unofficial songbooks such as *The Cokesbury Worship Hymnal*,[25] used by some congregations for the Sunday service and by many others for Sunday school, evening, or midweek worship.

The increasingly general use of worship bulletins designed for a particular congregation's use on a particular Sunday made it easy to tailor services to local wishes. While some affluent congregations continued to use bulletins that came out of a print shop, most congregations now mimeographed their bulletins. While many pastors used *The Book of Worship* (1945 and 1965) as a resource, attempts to get Methodist congregations to use a book of worship in the pews utterly failed. It was too easy to copy acts of worship from any available source into the bulletin.

There was general complacency about Sunday worship as this era drew to a close. Changes during the nineteenth and twentieth centuries had been gradual, and both those who preferred more formal worship and those who preferred less formal worship were settled into their own traditions. Diversity and discontents seemed quite manageable. Church membership had still been growing, and church unions were creating larger denominations. Three Methodist denominations united in 1939 to form The Methodist Church; The Evangelical Church and the United Brethren united in 1946 to form The Evangelical United Brethren Church; and these denominations in turn united in 1968 to form The United Methodist Church.

AN AGE OF CHANGE AND DIVERSITY

In 1968 the newly-formed United Methodist Church suddenly found itself facing a rapidly changing world that challenged the old assumptions about Sunday worship. Enough was already evident in 1968 that the denomination began the twenty-four-year process of rethinking and development that led to *The United Methodist Hymnal* (1989) and *The United Methodist Book of Worship* (1992). Throughout that process, and since these books were published, the world has continued to change rapidly.

United Methodists, historically so closely identified with American culture, have felt keenly the culture shocks that have rocked American society since the 1960s. Whatever divides Americans is likely to divide United Methodists, and matters related to worship such as language and musical styles have been the focus of many conflicts. The denomination has sought unity and inclusiveness in its diversity, and a major goal in the development of the 1989 *Hymnal* and 1992 *Book of Worship* was to make them inclusive and a means of unity among United Methodists.

Increasing American cultural diversity and secularism have led many United Methodists and other Christians to a feeling of growing distance from the culture that has been called "cultural disestablishment." This feeling has been all the stronger because since the 1960s "mainline" Protestant—including United Methodist—church membership has declined not only in proportion to the total population but also in absolute numbers, while at the same time increasing in average age. Some have suggested that Christians today may have more in common with the early Christians than with Christians in the intervening centuries when theirs was the established religion. Some United Methodists have begun to feel a renewed identification with the Methodist movement in the days of the Wesleys and Asbury, before it became prosperous and respectable.

In the midst of these struggles United Methodists have become more aware of the richness of their heritage. Former Methodists and former Evangelical United Brethren have shared their heritages. African American, Asian American, Hispanic, and Native American United Methodists have been remembering, reaffirming, and in many cases reclaiming, their own diverse heritages and sharing these heritages with other United Methodists. United Methodists are more aware of the historical contributions of women and more open to their contributions today. The charismatic movement and the liturgical movement have opened up diverse new possibilities for worship renewal. Scholars have given United Methodists a much fuller understanding of the Wesleys and our early American forebears, plus an understanding of how much of their heritage was gradually lost and forgotten during the nineteenth and twentieth centuries. Scholars of all denominations have given Christians a much better understanding of worship in the Bible, in the early church, and in later centuries.

Meanwhile, worship has been changing in other Christian denominations. Roman Catholic worship changed radically after the Second Vatican Council. Other Protestant and Anglican denominations have made major reforms in their official worship resources. Evangelical and charismatic congregations have been moving from traditional to contemporary styles of informal worship. There has been an explosion of Christian musical creativity in an incredible diversity of styles that reflects the diversity of contemporary secular music. We have learned from one another's experiences, and to an unprecedented degree worked together in the development of new resources.

Technology has also been opening up new possibilities in worship. Electronics has radically been changing music, in churches as in secular society. Church bulletins of superior quality can now easily and inexpensively be produced by word processing, desktop publishing, and photocopying. Services can be not only broadcast but telecast. Projection and video have increasingly been used.

All these changes have produced controversy, not only within United Methodism but within congregations. In many communities where there are two or more United Methodist congregations, these congregations have become differentiated from one another in large measure by their worship styles. In congregations that are able to have two or more weekly services, these increasingly are different in style so as to meet the needs of different segments of the congregation or community.

It is sometimes said that these worship styles are basically two, *traditional* and *alternative* (or *contemporary*); but matters are not that simple.

What does traditional mean? For one congregation it may be a service based on Morning Prayer and Sermon in a sanctuary with a divided chancel. For another it may be a praise service followed by preaching and invitation in a sanctuary with a central pulpit. For still another it may be a pattern introduced ten or twenty years ago as contemporary that has now become familiar and therefore traditional. It usually means "what we are used to doing."

What do contemporary or alternative mean? Some persons, when they hear these terms, think of a group seated in a large circle in the church social hall surrounded by banners and other homemade artifacts, "celebrating life" with a combination of sacred and secular readings and music and doing a snake dance or sending up balloons. Others think of people seated facing an open platform on which the performance of contemporary gospel or secular music and perhaps a short drama are followed by an informal Christian message that addresses the life situation evoked by the music and drama. Still others think of a small group seated around a coffee or dining table in someone's home, with informal conversation about their concerns and the claims of Christian faith followed by an informal contemporary celebration of the Lord's Supper. Whatever else these terms suggest, they generally indicate that the speaking and musical styles are informal and contemporary.

Even traditional services have tended to become livelier and more festive since the 1960s. Organ and piano have increasingly been joined by other acoustic and electronic instruments. A wider variety of traditional and contemporary music is sung, some of it to the beat of rhythms that would have been shocking in those sanctuaries a generation ago. Applause, formerly taboo, is now commonplace. In some churches "amens" and other spontaneous responses from the congregation are reappearing or becoming more frequent. Brightly colored paraments, banners, and other hangings now provide a festive visual environment in many a "traditional" sanctuary.

What is most notable about United Methodist sanctuaries built or remodeled since the 1960s may well be their diversity. Some, as in previous generations, have platforms with large central pulpits or chancels with altars against the wall. Many others have moved to a sanctuary design more appropriate to worship as they now understand it.

Newer sanctuary designs have tended to be simple and flexible. On the front platform the pulpit, Lord's Table, and other furnishings are often movable rather than fastened down. Sometimes congregational seating is also movable. Even the front platform itself may be in sections that can be moved. An arrangement of furnishings that is appropriate for a congregation's customary Sunday morning service may not be appropriate for a concert, a special program, or another style of worship. Seating can be adjusted as more or less attendance is expected.

The design of the sanctuary and the arrangement of furnishings for worship tend more clearly than in the previous generation to signify the priesthood of the whole congregation and enable greater congregational participation. The sanctuary is clearly one room rather than a combination of nave and chancel. The congregation is likely to sit in a curved, slightly v-shaped, or even wraparound fashion that minimizes their distance from the worship leaders and makes them more aware of the other worshipers. The Lord's Table usually looks like a table instead of an altar, and while it is probably central it has been moved out from the wall in order to be freestanding and closer to the people and so that the pastor can stand behind it facing the people. The pulpit is likely to be to one side if there is a center aisle, but the lectern on the other side may have given way to a baptismal font. The placement of choirs, while varying, tends to make them more a part of the congregation than they were when seated in the chancel facing the altar.

Clergywomen have been leading United Methodist worship far more commonly in the past generation, and they have often brought new perspectives and styles to congregational worship.

There has also been a great increase in the use of laypersons, both men and women, to assist the pastor in leading worship, particularly in congregations that have only one ordained minister.

Worshipers and their leaders have been as diverse in what they wear as in other respects. It is still customary in many congregations to come to worship in one's Sunday best, particularly at services that are perceived as traditional; but casual dress is encouraged in many other congregations and at alternative services. A great many choirs, soloists, and instrumentalists are robed in any of a variety of colors; but many others dress like the rest of the congregation. Lay worship leaders generally dress like the rest of the congregation, as do many clergy. While black clergy robes and conservative "preacher suits" from earlier eras are still common, so are newer vestments in a wide variety of styles and colors. Perhaps the most common new vestment is a white or light neutral-colored alb, widely worn ecumenically and appropriate for laypersons as well as clergy. Clergy stoles have become much more common.

Finally, as the society has become more religiously diverse and secular, more and more seekers with little or no knowledge of Christianity are searching for meaning in their lives. What they encounter if they visit the services of many congregations may seem to them irrelevant to their needs. There may also be cultural differences between them and the congregation they visit that have nothing to do with the essentials of the Christian gospel. They may need special ministries and perhaps special services designed for their needs. Perhaps such services should not even be worship services, though they might contain moments of worship. Yet changing regular congregational worship services to meet their needs might estrange the existing congregation, whose needs are very different.

With so much diversity in United Methodist worship, what is the basis of our unity? There has been a strong and growing call back to basics, back to our roots, back to the Bible as our surest source of unity. In many congregations more scripture is being read and preaching has become more biblical—a trend facilitated by the wide popularity of the ecumenical lectionary since the 1970s. In many congregations the Lord's Supper is being celebrated more frequently. There has been a growing conviction among United Methodists that if we can see and experience a basic unity behind our diversity, we can not only live with this diversity but find in it a source of life and strength. It is this conviction that guided the development of the 1989 *Hymnal* and the 1992 *Book of Worship* and the Basic Pattern of Worship that is at their heart.

WORSHIP RESOURCES FOR A NEW DAY

Underlying the development of this hymnal and *Book of Worship* were several fundamental assumptions.

These resources were designed primarily for the regular weekly worship services of congregations that are Christian and United Methodist. It was assumed that hospitality and sensitivity to visitors from other congregations and denominations and to seekers of any or no religious affiliation is essential and is entirely consistent with the full and uncompromising ministry of Word and Sacrament needed by faithful Christians. It was assumed that visitors and seekers who take the trouble to attend a congregational worship service want to know who we are and what we stand for, and they have a right to the full truth up-front.

To be sure, meetings designed primarily for seekers and dealing with their distinctive concerns are also needed and require resources beyond what were included in the hymnal and *Book of Worship*. Such resources are needed and must be based on a comprehensive strategy for nurturing seekers step-by-step into the fullness of Christian faith and life. The development of such a strategy, with appropriate resources, will take time and is increasingly a priority among United Methodists and ecumenically.

It is evident that no one-size-fits-all approach can be developed for ministries with seekers. Because seekers are diverse, what is right for one seeker may be wrong for another. Some meetings for seekers may appropriately be services of worship—or at least include acts of worship—and use the hymnal, *Book of Worship*, or other worship resources. Other such meetings may more appropriately consist of secular or Christian music, drama, teaching, or informal conversation in a context other than worship. The setting might be a church sanctuary, a church social hall or classroom, a theatre, an auditorium, an office, or someone's home. Often it is important that it be held in what seekers perceive as "neutral territory," free of any Christian symbols or associations.

But if seekers are diverse, so are the United Methodist Christians who now worship week after week. It was recognized that we need unity in our diversity, if we are to retain any identity as United Methodists, and the Basic Pattern of Worship was set at the beginning of the hymnal and *Book of Worship* to show that there is a simple and flexible unifying pattern in our weekly worship.

The Basic Pattern of Worship consists of four parts: (1) entrance, (2) proclamation and response, (3) thanksgiving and communion, and (4) sending forth. The "outer" parts (1 and 4) are the opening and closing, which are essential parts of congregational worship services, as they are of any meeting. The "inner" parts (2 and 3), as we have seen from our biblical and historical survey, are the core of the service.

Immediately following the Basic Pattern of Worship section in the hymnal (3-5) and *Book of Worship* (16-32) is An Order of Sunday Worship Using the Basic Pattern, "showing some of the variety that is possible within the Basic Pattern of Worship." To achieve a balance of freedom and order, the Basic Pattern of Worship needs to be fleshed out to give more specific and practical help in ordering services:

> While the freedom and diversity of United Methodist worship are greater than can be represented by any single order of worship, United Methodists also affirm a heritage of order and the importance of the specific guidance and modeling that an order of worship provides. (*BOW* 16)

An Order of Sunday Worship uses the indefinite article in its title to acknowledge that it is not necessarily the most appropriate order of worship for every congregation, but it provides a historic and ecumenical order as a model:

> Like the Basic Pattern, it is a guide to help those who plan worship see the structure and flow of our services. It is not intended that the congregation follow pages 3-5 in the hymnal

while at worship. The congregation may be guided through
the service by a bulletin or by announcement.   (*BOW* 16)

The commentary on each item in An Order of Sunday Worship gives specific ideas for planning services.

Both the Basic Pattern and An Order of Sunday Worship make it clear that the service by its very structure is to be a unity and thereby a witness to the church's unity of purpose. There is one Basic Pattern, whether or not the Lord's Supper is being celebrated. The Lord's Supper is neither an add-on to the usual Sunday service nor a service whose pattern from beginning to end is different from other Sunday services. It is the fullest expression of the Basic Pattern that is followed at every service. Preaching is not to be deemphasized when the Lord's Supper follows but is fully as important then as at any other service. Word and Table strengthen each other. It is recognized that most United Methodist congregations today do not celebrate "the supper of the Lord on every Lord's day" as John Wesley advocated, but the Basic Pattern points and helps them toward that ideal.

When the Lord's Supper is not celebrated, Sunday worship is a Service of the Word. This is a more faithful and fruitful interpretation, both of Wesley's Sunday Service and of our preaching service heritage as outlined in *Disciplines* beginning in 1792, than was the attempt during the past century or so to make Sunday worship into an adaptation of Anglican Morning Prayer and Sermon. On the one hand, Morning Praise and Prayer is recognized as an essential service in its own right and made part of a revived Orders of Daily Prayer (*UMH* 876-879; *BOW* 568-580) rather than being made, in awkward combination and tension with preaching, the main Sunday service. On the other hand, a Service of the Word is a unity in which entrance leads naturally to proclamation and the sermon closely follows scripture so as to encourage and strengthen biblical preaching.

But worship services are far more than overall patterns and orders. They are the interaction of God with the gathered congregation—an interaction that can take many forms and often be spontaneous and unpredictable but that for United Methodists most often takes place through words, music, and symbolic actions such as receiving the offering or sharing in the Lord's Supper. Specific acts of worship can be clear channels for the Spirit, or they can be barriers. As the saying goes, God and the devil are both in the details. This is why the choosing of specific texts, music, and acts to flesh out an order of worship and create a service should be done with great care.

After the initial Basic Pattern and Order of Sunday Worship, the rest of the hymnal and *Book of Worship* is a treasury of specific texts, music, and services for use in United Methodist worship. Every one of these was carefully examined by many people before being included in these official books. Many prayers, hymns and songs, phrases, even individual words were fiercely argued over as the task of determining what was to be included in these books was taken seriously and responsibly by all concerned.

Though it was recognized that while the hymnal and *Book of Worship* are not books of church law and have no authority to command or forbid anything, they have great permission-giving and enabling power. Including an act or Service of Worship in these officially authorized books has the double effect of legitimating it and making it convenient for United Methodist use. By looking at all the specific acts of worship as well as at the overall patterns and orders in the hymnal and *Book of Worship* we see what these books taken as a whole say to United Methodists.

They are a strong reaffirmation of our biblical and Wesleyan heritage and of our doctrinal standards and theological task as set forth in the *Discipline* (1992, Part II, pp. 40-86). Anyone planning worship services in United Methodist congregations or wondering what is the doctrinal basis of the hymnal and *Book of Worship* can profitably study this part of the *Discipline*. In it The United Methodist Church officially expresses its fundamental beliefs and describes how it (the

General Conference) goes about its continuing theological task. In worship as in theological reflection, scripture is primary; and tradition, experience, and reason also play essential roles.

The recognition that scripture is primary is reflected in the greater prominence of scripture in worship as well as in a determination to be faithful to the teachings of scripture. This is most plainly seen in the emphasis on scripture readings, Psalter, and biblical preaching. It is also present in the innumerable words, images, and teachings from scripture that saturate the prayers, hymns, and songs.

In the hymnal and *Book of Worship*, as in the *Discipline*, biblical and Wesleyan orthodoxy is a living, growing tradition, not a static system. These books represent an earnest attempt to combine authenticity with relevance and orthodoxy with inclusiveness, in faithfulness to scripture, to the teachings held in common by the ecumenical church, and to both the Methodist and Evangelical United Brethren branches of our Wesleyan heritage.

This approach is seen, for example, in the concern throughout these books for a fuller and more balanced trinitarian faith in an age when the doctrine of the Trinity is poorly understood and under attack from many quarters. The biblical terms "Father" and "Lord" are repeatedly used and strongly reaffirmed, while at the same time other names for God and for Jesus Christ that are scriptural or in harmony with scripture are also used. The work of the Holy Spirit receives much more recognition. There is a more balanced celebration of God's work of creation, redemption, sanctification, and ultimate victory over evil, recognizing that each of these is the work of the whole Trinity.

This emphasis on proclaiming and celebrating the *whole* gospel—*all* of God's good news—brings a new accent on joyful praise and thanksgiving throughout these books. This involves more than joyful words. The music, the actions, the pace of the whole service are all livelier.

¶ 74

The acts of worship in these books come from more diverse sources than ever before. There are far more hymns, prayers, and other acts of worship from African American, Asian American, Hispanic, and Native American sources. A wider variety of nations is represented. Hymn stanzas and other acts of worship occasionally use languages other than English. There are more contributions by women. These acts of worship are commended not only for the segments of the church in which they originated but for use by all United Methodists.

This diversity is a reminder that when we worship we are joined, visibly or invisibly, by "a great multitude that no one could count, from every nation, from all tribes and peoples and languages" (Rev. 7:9). When we use a language or a musical style not our own in worship we are reminded that God understands all languages. We are also reminded that the native language of the Church is the language that the Bible (Acts 2:1-11) tells us was spoken on the day the Church was born—all languages mutually understood. We anticipate the conversation at the heavenly feast.

In this inclusive spirit, great effort was made to avoid language or assumptions that are insensitive or discriminatory with respect to women, to persons of any age or stage of development, to any racial or ethnic group, or to persons with disabilities. One statement in the introduction to An Order of Sunday Worship deserves to be quoted here and taken to heart by all planners of worship:

> As Jesus invited children to come to him, so United Methodist worship should welcome children and youth as an integral part of the community as participants in, and leaders of, worship. Congregational worship services should include stories, songs and other music, and actions that are appropriate to children and youth of various ages and abilities. (*BOW* 16)

Finally, there is more openness to the unexpected workings of the Spirit in worship now and in the future. Spontaneous expressions of many sorts are recognized and encouraged.

There is more affirmation of creativity on the part of those who plan and lead worship. There is an overall recognition that in the lifetime of these books United Methodist worship is likely to change in ways that those who worked to produce these books could not possibly have predicted.

All of this follows naturally from the understanding of worship as encounter that was expressed earlier in this book. So far we have been looking at the worship service as a whole, as those who plan and lead United Methodist worship must do. But they must also plan and lead worship item by item. We shall now go in sequence through the parts of the Basic Pattern and ask how each act of worship can be most effective and best contribute to the overall flow of the service.

CHAPTER 5

Entrance

✝

GATHERING

Once upon a time, a Quaker brought a friend to join him in silent worship at the Quaker meetinghouse. Not knowing the ways of the Quakers, the friend was puzzled when he saw the assembled people sitting in silence. After a while he whispered to his host, "When does the service begin?" His host replied, "When the meeting has ended."

This story reminds us of two important truths:

1) What we call a service of worship is a *meeting*, an assembly, a gathering in which we encounter God and one another. This is literally what the biblical words that we translate *church* and *synagogue* both mean. The word *congregation* is derived from a Latin verb meaning "to flock together" and means essentially the same thing. Not only Quakers but also many other Christians, including early Methodists, have used the terms *meeting* and *meetinghouse.*

2) Worship in the broadest sense of the word—our participation with the rest of creation in an ongoing encounter with God—is continuous, without beginning or end. When we participate in the life of a worshiping congregation there is the pulsating rhythm, week after week, of gathering (meeting) and scattering (service). Sometimes, such as for Sunday worship,

we are the gathered church. Most of the time we are the church scattered for life and service in the wider world.

Of course, congregational meetings for worship are also a form of service, an offering to God and a support for one another. It is not wrong to speak of a worship *service* as long as we remember that it is a meeting for worship.

So let's ask, "When does the service begin?" When does it begin in the experience of the worshipers? When in that experience is the first moment planners of worship should be planning?

Many people assume that the service begins with the first words spoken to the assembled congregation from up-front or with an opening hymn or introit, whichever comes first. This impression is reinforced by the bulletin when these are the first items listed in the order of worship, or when those first words are termed a "call to worship," or possibly even when the instrumental music offered to God prior to that time is called a "prelude"—as if it were preservice music.

It is a significant step forward when that prior music is recognized as an act of worship, both in the church bulletin and by the attitudes and actions of the congregation. This has long been done in the orders of worship in our official hymnals and books of worship.

The present hymnal and *Book of Worship* have taken a further step forward by recognizing that the service begins even earlier. If the worship service is a *meeting* for worship, then it begins when the congregation first meet one another—when, in the words of the Basic Pattern, "the people come together in the Lord's name." This time of coming together, entitled "Gathering," is the first act of worship listed in An Order of Sunday Worship (*UMH* 3; *BOW* 16-17).

This time needs to be as carefully planned as any other part of the service. It is experienced by worshipers as part of the service. I have long since learned from visiting churches that what happens during the Gathering is an astonishingly accurate indicator of how much—or little—vitality there will be in the rest of the service.

Because the term "gathering" and its underlying idea are new to most United Methodists, both the hymnal and especially the *Book of Worship* spell out in detail what may take place during this time. These explanations will repay careful study. But first, let's put ourselves into the place of someone coming to our weekly service, whether as a member like Jack Smith or as a visitor like Jean Jones.

In the Gathering, as throughout the service, there is a constant interplay of call and response. Something served as a means by which what we trust was God's call has got through to each person who makes the effort to attend.

With Jack Smith, the church member, it may be force of habit (which can be God's way of calling him) or, since he is divorced, may be a thought like: "The kids are with me this weekend; maybe I'd better take them to church" (which also can be God's call). He responds to this call by getting himself and the children ready for church, everyone dressed in what he knows are the customary clothes (the Sunday-go-to-meeting clothes, to use the quaint old phrase) for that congregation, and herding everyone into the car. In the process he is running late and has got himself into something of a frazzle.

Jean Jones is not only a visitor but also an unchurched seeker. She is going through a hard time in her life, feels the need for support, and thinks maybe a church could help (which can be God's call). A friend mentioned having heard that this particular congregation was understanding and helpful but was not a member and did not offer to bring her, though that would have made her visit much easier. She looked up the congregation's address in the phone directory and called the church Saturday afternoon for the time of the service, which since the church office was closed she got from a recorded message. Not knowing what to wear for church, she acted on the hunch that it was better to overdress than be too casual. She nervously drove to the church alone, allowing herself plenty of time because she didn't know how long it would take to get there and find a parking space.

For both of them the meeting—the service—began when they first met another worshiper in the parking lot.

Jean arrived early, as visitors often do, but didn't know where the parking lot was. As she passed the church she saw a sign directing her to the parking lot around the corner and behind the church. When she rounded the corner she saw a volunteer attendant, who gestured her into a parking space, greeted her when she got out of the car, and gave her directions to the sanctuary. Although the door from her end of the parking lot was not the main door of the church, she was further reassured to see a sign immediately inside the door giving directions not only to the sanctuary but to the rest rooms and child care facilities as well. She went to the women's room, then toward the sanctuary.

Jack arrived a little late, worried that there would be no good parking left, wondering how far he would have to walk with his young children, and remembering the days when his former wife would have taken the children into church while he hunted for parking. Fortunately the attendant spotted the children in the car with him, beckoned to an incredibly good space near the handicap spaces, and reminded him that the church had reserved spaces near the door for single parents. He walked the few steps to the door, saw the directions to child care facilities, and decided to take the younger child there before going with the older child toward the sanctuary.

As Jean approached the sanctuary and began encountering other people she was pleasantly surprised by the many people who greeted her warmly. She fell into conversation with another single woman, who invited her to sit with her in church and helped her find her way in the bulletin and hymnal during the service. She liked the service and was pleased at how easy it was to follow with the help of her newfound friend.

As Jack and his child approached the sanctuary a few minutes late, a greeter welcomed both of them and then an usher whose manner assured them that their being late was no problem, quietly and inconspicuously seated them at an appropriate moment.

For both Jean and Jack what happened before they even entered the sanctuary set the tone for the whole service.

Every congregation needs systematically to plan this gathering time, thinking step-by-step through what every person will experience coming to that church—regular members, visitors from other churches, unchurched seekers, those who wish sociability, those who wish privacy, persons with every sort of disability. More and clearer signs may be needed. The building may need to be altered by additions such as ramps, elevators, wider doorways and aisles, and space for wheelchairs in the sanctuary. Determine the best ways of enabling persons with every degree of hearing or visual impairment to participate in the worship. Train greeters and ushers in effective hospitality, particularly to persons with special needs.

The most important—and most difficult—requirement is that the congregation as a whole make effective hospitality a priority. I have often been a visitor in congregations where many people, not just designated greeters, greeted me with obvious hospitality, even when they could not have been sure whether I was a visitor or a church member they didn't know. This hospitality does not just happen. It happens when a congregation is led and educated to make it a priority. It also helps when the worship as a whole is so vital that church members are happy to come, joyous at the end of the service, and eager to share the joy of that worship with others.

The people need to be called to remember that they are coming together *in the Lord's name.* A church bell or bells or amplified music may remind the gathering people who they are and why they are coming together. The sight of the church building is also a reminder. Persons on their way from an outer door to the inner sanctuary door commonly go through an entrance room or space, sometimes called the *narthex,* where people can not only greet one another and renew their sense of community but also be reminded that they are making a major transition as they come from the outside world to a sanctuary consecrated to a sacred purpose and filled with sacred associations.

There is not only an outward and visible gathering of the people, there is also an inward and spiritual gathering—a "getting it all together." As we saw from Jack's and Jean's experiences, people have all kinds of preoccupations as they come to church. They need to put aside their preoccupations and become centered. The congregation that gathers physically needs also to gather spiritually (center) into a focused awareness that they are a people gathered in the presence of the living God known to us through Jesus Christ in the power of the Holy Spirit.

The Gathering includes not only what happens as people are entering the place of worship but also what happens after they are seated. Inside the sanctuary they are surrounded by a multitude of visual reminders that call them to remember who they are and why they are here. It is here, as the congregation is outwardly and visibly gathering in their seats, that much of the inward and spiritual gathering (centering) is also taking place. In those congregations where worship immediately follows another activity in the sanctuary such as Sunday school, and when some persons who have been at the earlier activity simply remain seated for the worship that follows, there needs to be a time for this inward and spiritual gathering.

It should be acknowledged that the same symbol-filled sanctuary that is a supportive environment for the worshiping congregation can seem forbidding to some unchurched seekers, because it is either strange and alien or else filled with bad associations from the past. Meetings designed primarily for such seekers may intentionally be held in secular settings, often without any visible Christian symbols such as crosses, altars, or banners, or in some other room of a church building. They can constitute for the seeker a halfway house on the way to full participation in the worshiping congregation. When seekers first attend congregational worship, it is very helpful to be accompanied by a church member who can interpret what is happening and be a reassuring presence.

It should also be acknowledged that what should happen in the sanctuary during the Gathering is often the subject of intense controversy within a worship committee. An organist offering a musical act of worship during the Gathering and those who wish to listen or meditate may clash with those who wish to have conversation with friends seated around them in the sanctuary. There is much to be said for rehearsing unfamiliar hymns and other congregational music and acts of worship, making necessary announcements, and welcoming visitors during the latter part of the Gathering after the people are assembled; but this also may be controversial.

The *Book of Worship* (17) lists six types of activity that often take place during the Gathering, together with ways in which these may be combined. Those who plan a congregation's worship might reflect on this statement and determine what pattern is most appropriate for them.

In most United Methodist congregations people entering the sanctuary for congregational worship receive a printed bulletin containing announcements and the order of worship for that service. With the use of present-day multimedia computers and copying machines these bulletins can be as attractive and readable as if they came out of a print shop. A booklet such as David A. Wiltse's *Your Ministry of Designing the Worship Bulletin* (Nashville: Discipleship Resources, 1991) and the advice of an experienced designer or copy center in your community can help. Visitors and seekers are likely to look at the bulletin as soon as they take their seats, and what they see there is likely to affect how they feel about that congregation.

Many persons need or prefer a bulletin with very large and bold print on unfolded sheets, which can be stapled together if more than one sheet is required. These can be run off in whatever quantity is needed in addition to the regular folded bulletin. Some congregations, especially if they are predominantly older persons, now print all their bulletins in large and bold type.

There are special moments when leaders of worship enter the Gathering.

The pastor(s) can enter at various times and in various ways. Some prefer to enter and take their seats silently and inconspicuously at some point in the Gathering. Others enter to stand in front of the congregation for informal moments of greeting, welcoming of visitors, necessary announcements, and rehearsal of unfamiliar acts of worship. Some choose to be outside or inside the sanctuary greeting the congregation one by one as they enter. These pastors may find that they have a more natural and unhurried chance to greet people as they enter than is the case after the service when there is a long line of persons waiting to shake hands with the pastor or greeters. Still other pastors enter later as part of the procession that will be discussed below.

The organist or other instrumentalist(s) may be the first of the leaders to enter. As Psalm 150 affirms, instrumental music can be a traditional and appropriate offering of praise to God, during the Gathering and at other times in the service as well. A congregation by its attitude can indicate that they are participating in this act of worship. Any such musical offerings should, if possible, be listed in the church bulletin. A term such as "musical offering," "organ meditation," or "voluntary" indicates more clearly than "prelude" that this is an act of worship. Such an offering is likely to be most effective *after* any conversation or informal moments that have occurred earlier in the Gathering. It can serve as a fitting transition from the informality of the earlier gathering to the more formal acts of corporate praise and prayer that follow.

The choir may enter and be seated quietly at some point during the Gathering or enter as a singing procession to open the corporate praise and prayer that follows.

A worship leader other than the pastor and musicians may enter quietly with the pastor and be seated during the Gathering, may enter as part of a procession, or may be seated in the midst of the congregation and come forward for whatever part of the service he or she will be leading.

If candles are used during the service they may be ceremonially lighted by one or two persons commonly called *acolytes* or *servers,* either during the Gathering or immediately after they have come forward with the procession. While adults may serve in this ministry, it is an especially good way of giving older children and youth a more active role in worship. Congregations can use Michael O'Donnell's booklet *Your Ministry of Being an Acolyte* or my booklet *The Acolyte's Book* (both listed under Additional Resources) in training persons for this ministry.

Some or all of these persons may be wearing robes or vestments. As was mentioned above, there is a wide variety of clothing worn today by United Methodist leaders of worship. An academic robe, sometimes worn with a hood, signifies a pastor's educational preparation and teaching ministry. A white or light neutral-colored alb, adapted from the basic garment worn by men and women alike in the early days of Christianity, is a link with the early Christians and signifies the presence of the whole communion of saints—the "great multitude . . . robed in white" (Rev. 7:9). Albs may properly be worn by laypersons as well as by clergy. On the other hand, the stole has from ancient times signified that the wearer is ordained. None of these vestments is necessary, however; and the less formal the service the less likely it is that any of them will be worn.

PRAISE AND PRAYER

The Gathering, together with the next acts in the service that we shall now examine, form the first major part of the service, known as the *Entrance*. Some have called the Entrance the *Approach* or the *Preparation*. The Basic Pattern of Worship describes it with these words: "The people come together in the Lord's name. There may be greetings, music and song, prayer and praise." This description calls to mind Psalm 100: "Come into [God's] presence with singing! . . . Enter [God's] gates with thanksgiving, and [God's] courts with praise."

The people are not simply entering the place of worship, they are also entering into an encounter with the living God, through the risen Christ, in the power of the Holy Spirit. The Entrance should bring the congregation, individually and corporately, to full, conscious, focused participation in this encounter so that they will be ready to hear the Word of God proclaimed.

A major turning point in the middle of the Entrance occurs when the pastor, choir, or other leaders of worship begin speaking or singing in such a manner as to draw the whole congregation into a call-and-response sequence in which the people are in audible dialogue with God and with one another in the Lord's name. The term "the Lord" means both the Lord God and the Lord Jesus Christ. We are called together in the name of the God revealed in Jesus Christ. What comes next in the service is predominantly a time of praise and prayer. Some refer to it as the praise service. In some congregations it is mainly a song service. The *Book of Worship* (17-22) provides a wealth of detailed help for this part of the service.

This praise and prayer can begin in different ways. In some orders of worship the leader greets the people in the Lord's name and calls them to praise God, and the people respond by greeting God with a hymn or song of praise. In other orders the hymn or song of praise comes first, during which the choir, pastor, and other worship leaders may enter in a procession and after which a leader faces the people, greets them in the Lord's name, and calls them to some further response such as prayer. Sometimes the choir also sings what may be called an *introit*, which may call the congregation to praise or be itself an act of praise.

The leader's greeting to the congregation should be face-to-face and explicitly Christian, given in the Lord's name and making it clear that the Lord is present and empowers the congregation's worship. A secular greeting such as "good morning" may be suitable earlier for introducing informal moments during the Gathering, but it does not say what needs to be said here and tends to trivialize what is happening. As the examples in the *Book of Worship* (18) illustrate, the greeting may be either a scripture sentence or a simple and easily memorized responsive act of greeting that if used over a period of time could become as natural as an exchange of "good morning." Alternatively, there may be an informal spoken greeting, but it is more than a secular greeting and should be explicitly in the Lord's name. In some congregations there is a different responsive exchange printed in the bulletin every week, often longer and more complicated than the simple example in the *Book of Worship*. This provides variety, but it keeps the people's eyes glued to the bulletin and makes it seem less like a face-to-face greeting. In any event, the greeting should not be referred to as a "call to worship," since using that term here would imply that the Gathering had not been part of the worship. If there is a choir introit, it should be *in addition to*, not instead of, the greeting by the leader. "*Leader* means a worship leader, who may be either lay or clergy," whenever it is used in the *Book of Worship* (12).

Processions may take place every Sunday or only on especially festive occasions. Customarily the pastor is at the end of the procession, following the choir(s) and any assisting worship leader(s). If acolytes have not lit the candles during the Gathering they may lead the procession and then light the candles. More elaborate processions may be led by a *crucifer* (cross carrier), two *torchbearers*, and *banner* or *flag bearers* in that order. These may be acolytes. The processional cross, torches (large lighted candles), banners, and flags are fastened onto staffs or poles for carrying and are placed in platform or chancel stands during the service. The rhythm of a processional hymn should be appropriate for walking, but the procession should not attempt to keep in step with it as if it were a march. The hymn should be long enough for the completion of the procession.

It is appropriate for the congregation to stand for the singing of the opening hymn. If the hymn precedes the greeting, it is appropriate to remain standing for the greeting. Here and everywhere in the service that standing is suggested, it is important to bear in mind the note in the *Book of Worship* (12) concerning those who cannot stand or have difficulty doing so. Also, local customs regarding when to stand should be taken into account. This is why suggestions regarding standing are found in the *Book of Worship* for consideration by planners and leaders of worship but are not found in the hymnal, where they might appear to be directing every congregation.

The suggestions regarding choice of an opening hymn, song, doxology, chorus, acclamation, or canticle (*BOW* 18-19) show some of the many possibilities. Of course, congregations are not limited to a single sung act of praise at this point. Several of these may be sung, one after the other, as an opening song service. A worship leader skilled in song leading can be particularly valuable if such a pattern is followed.

"Opening prayers, together with opening hymns, establish that our worship is communion with God as well as with one another. They include recognition of who we are before God by centering on the nature and gifts of God" (*BOW* 20). The *Book of Worship* has a helpful discussion of posture in public prayer, of congregational *amens*, and of several appropriate types of opening prayer.

Training a congregation to say or sing *amen* at the end of a prayer led by an individual significantly adds to the vitality of that congregation's worship. The biblical Hebrew word *amen* means "so be it" and expresses agreement with, and participation in, what has been said. A prayer spoken by one voice becomes the whole congregation's prayer with the people's *amen.* The choir should of course participate in the *amen* but should not take it away from the rest of the congregation. A congregation can more easily add an *amen* to prayers that end with a phrase they can recognize, such as "through Jesus Christ our Lord" or "in Jesus' name." A leader can give a cue for a congregational *amen* at any time in a service with words such as, "Let the church say," followed by the people's *amen.*

Amen and other expressions such as "yes" or "praise God," spontaneously spoken by persons in the congregation at any appropriate time in the service, make the call-and-response nature of worship highly audible and can add even more life to congregational worship. Such spontaneous responses were common in early American frontier worship and have continued in various segments of United Methodism to this day. Some congregations in recent years have been recovering and reclaiming this gift, but it cannot be forced on a congregation that experiences it as alien and unnatural. What the people say or sing from the bulletin or hymnal, their body language, and what goes on in their hearts are also legitimate responses in the call-and-response pattern that pervades worship.

Prayer can be sung as well as spoken. If a congregation has an opening song service, much of it may in fact be prayer. As the *Book of Worship* (20-21) points out, even a confession and pardon sequence can easily be sung.

There are other choices relating to confession and pardon. Should they be in this part of the service or a response to the Word? Some advantages of each are mentioned in the *Book of Worship* (21), and each has a long history in our United Methodist heritage. Prior to 1964 the confession and pardon were always after the proclamation of the Word when the Lord's Supper was celebrated, and this remained the pattern in the 1964 brief form of the Lord's Supper. On the other hand, the order of Sunday worship, which had not mentioned confession and pardon before 1932, began at that time to make provision for them near the opening of worship, following the pattern of Anglican Morning Prayer. Another option, though not mentioned in the hymnal or *Book of Worship*, is not to have confession and pardon every Sunday but save them for times like Lent or special occasions such as healing services when they can be emphasized and perhaps seem less routine. If this option is taken, care should be exercised to see that in the prayers or other acts of worship every Sunday there is acknowledgment that we are sinners saved by grace.

A congregation can pray by means other than speech or song. Times of silent prayer, especially following confession, are part of many United Methodist worship services. Through interpretive movement or sacred dance, one person or a few persons or a whole congregation may pray in body language, either in silence or while words of prayer are being spoken or sung.

Standing, kneeling, bowing one's head, looking up, or closing one's eyes while praying are forms of prayer in body language. In biblical times and in the ancient church people stood for prayer, and congregations often do today (1 Sam. 1:26; Matt. 6:5; Mark 11:25; Luke 18:11). Sometimes the leader, and perhaps others in the congregation as well, add the biblical raising of outstretched hands, especially in prayers of praise or thanksgiving (1 Kings 8:22; Pss. 28:2, 63:4, 134:2, 141:2; Isa. 1:15; Lam. 2:19, 3:41; 1 Tim. 2:8). Other persons and congregations kneel, especially for prayers of confession. Still others remain seated, perhaps bowing their heads and sitting straight and alert. Some persons pray most naturally with their eyes closed, others with their eyes open. One posture is not necessarily correct and the others wrong; persons and congregations are free to decide what posture goes best with their prayer to God.

Congregations of the deaf worship in sign language. In many other congregations someone signs what is said or sung—that is, interprets it in sign language—not only for those who cannot hear but because many persons who can hear the words find that signing adds another dimension to spoken acts of worship.

Opening prayers may be followed by another act of praise. This may take any of several forms mentioned in the *Book of Worship* (21-22). The congregation may sing or speak praise in the form of a hymn, stanza, song, chorus, doxology, psalm, canticle, or litany. The "Lord, Have Mercy" in threefold form (*UMH* 482) and the "Canticle of God's Glory" (*UMH* 72, 82, or 83) have traditionally been sung at this point in services of Word and Table, while the Gloria Patri has been sung at this point in Morning Prayer. The form of praise that is now most commonly found at this point in United Methodist churches is a choir anthem.

This is a good point to remember the discussion above (pp. 21-22) concerning the functions of a choir and the relationship between choir and congregation. Taking leadership in worship is far more than giving a performance. It is a ministry that depends for its effectiveness upon being in tune both with the spirit of worship and with the needs of the congregation.

Several additional acts of worship that are suggested in the *Book of Worship* for other points in the service can instead be included in the Entrance if desired.

Congregations that do not wish to place the Concerns and Prayers and the Offering after the Proclamation of the Word may place them at the Opening Prayers and Praise in the service. The Opening Prayers may be expanded to include the Concerns and Prayers, with the Offering following, accompanied by an act of praise or by an organ or other instrumental voluntary. (*BOW* 25)

If announcements and welcoming are not placed in the Gathering, they may follow the Opening Prayers and Praise. (*BOW* 22)

If both these options are chosen, the announcements might be placed between the opening prayers and the offering.

Lay witnessing, drama, and sacred dance can be done here as well as later in the service, depending on their function and purpose in a particular service.

¶ *91*

This whole praise and prayer section of the service is summarized in An Order of Worship (*UMH* 3; *BOW* 17-22) as two items: GREETING AND HYMN and OPENING PRAYERS AND PRAISE. It resembles the items "singing" and "prayer" that preceded scripture reading and preaching in the early American Methodist directions for Sunday morning worship. If desired, this can be very brief: (1) greeting, (2) opening hymn, and (3) opening prayer. It can be longer but informal: (1) informal greeting, (2) song service, and (3) prayer. It can be more formal: (1) processional hymn, (2) greeting, (3) unison prayer of confession and pardon, and (4) anthem. It can include historic acts of praise that further link us to the ecumenical church. It can be extended as long as desired by doing more singing, expanding the prayer to become the main prayer of the service, by adding announcements and offering (with music) after the prayer, and by including other optional acts of worship.

As we have looked at all the different ways of conducting the opening service of praise and prayer, we may feel confused and wonder why we have all these choices. Couldn't the church simply dictate one pattern for all congregations? Here it helps to remember the basic function that the Entrance serves and how it relates to the proclamation and response that follows.

The *Book of Worship* interprets the Basic Pattern of Worship in the light of the Emmaus account in Luke 24:13-35. Of the Gathering it says:

> As on the first day of the week the two disciples were joined by the risen Christ, so in the power of the Holy Spirit the risen and ascended Christ joins us when we gather.　　(*BOW* 14)

Of the praise and prayer that follows the Gathering it continues:

> As the disciples poured out to him their sorrow and in so doing opened their hearts to what Jesus would say to them, so we

pour out to him whatever is on our hearts and thereby open
ourselves to the Word.   (*BOW* 14)

What is "on our hearts"? For those two disciples it was their
honest sharing of sorrow, disillusionment, doubt, and despair
that opened them to the Word. Later that evening, when they
returned to Jerusalem and "found the eleven and their com-
panions gathered together," it was their joyous and believing
sharing of the good news that opened their hearts to the Word
(Luke 24:36-49). In a second-century church under persecution, coming to a hasty secret meeting at the risk of one's life
could itself be preparation enough for hearing the Word.
Today, Christian congregations coming together in the faith
and power of the Holy Spirit are generally more like the
disciples in Jerusalem than like the two walking toward
Emmaus, which is why praise is so prominent in the Entrance.

But even today, "whatever is on our hearts" can be highly
diverse. We have sins and needs to acknowledge, even though
we may do so in faith. Some come with a faith that is weak, or
flickering, or lost. Some may never have heard the good news.
Some unbelieving seekers may be unchurched visitors, but
some may be members of the congregation.

What is on the hearts of the congregation may reflect either
the calendar or recent worldwide, national, or local events. Is
it Christmas or Easter? Is it the middle of a frigid, dreary
January or during a "summer slump" when half the congregation is away? Has there been great good news or a disaster in
the world around us since we last met? Are we meeting for the
first time in a brand new sanctuary? Are we meeting in temporary quarters because last week our church building was
devastated by a fire, earthquake, or tornado?

An appropriate length for the praise and prayer depends
in part on the Entrance customs of the people and the length
of the service as a whole. Is practically everyone assembled by
the time the opening hymn is sung, or will substantial numbers of people be coming in for some time after that? United
Methodist services can last forty-five minutes or less, or they

can last two hours or more. Those worshipers who want to do their duty and go home and those who are having the time of their lives because they *are* home are likely to have very different feelings about how long the service should last.

This part of the service should prepare the way for, and enhance, the proclamation of the Word. At the end of the praise and prayer the people should be ready for the Word. The praise and prayer should not normally be expanded to the point that they crowd or diminish the proclamation of the Word.

Most of the praise and prayer should be in the people's heart language—their musical as well as spoken heart language. People's heart language can expand as they come to be at home in new spoken and musical idioms, but this happens gradually and cannot be rushed. Praises and prayers that use archaic English, other languages, or musical styles not their own can represent for a congregation the unseen presence and contribution of the universal Church; but the core of *their* contribution to the worship of the universal Church should be in an idiom that is genuinely *theirs.*

We want music (our kind of music, of course) to be a universal language, but in our society music divides as well as unites. United Methodists are as diverse in their musical tastes when they praise God as they are when they go to concerts, listen to the radio, turn on the TV, or buy recordings. There are husbands and wives who attend different United Methodist congregations because they like different kinds of church music. If we inquire among the unchurched people in our community we are likely to find that their musical heart language is not what is usually heard in our congregation's worship. If they come to our services they are often put off rather than attracted by our church music.

Speaking in tongues is a spiritual gift (and another heart language) that some Christians have found to be a means of grace and ministry since New Testament times, but that other Christians have found disruptive and offensive. Paul's advice when he was confronted with this controversy (1 Cor. 12-14) is the definitive wisdom on the subject. It is significant that this controversy was the occasion for writing his famous "love chapter." Congregations that deal successfully with this issue are likely to do so by permitting the gift of tongues to be exercised at some weekly service *other than* the one attended by those who find it disruptive.

For all these reasons and more, there cannot be one style of worship for all United Methodist congregations. Congregations that can have two or more weekly services increasingly design these in differing styles so as to reach a wider range of people. The differences of style will affect the entire service but are likely to be especially prominent in the praise and prayer.

A congregation, whether it has one or more than one weekly service, should realistically assess its gifts and limitations and discern accordingly the ministries to which it is called. A large congregation with an excellent ministry of classical music is flourishing and attracting a great many new "baby boomer" and "generation X" members whom the senior pastor describes as part of the "traditionalist" or "loyalist" segments of their generations. Meanwhile, a new United Methodist congregation a few miles away in the same metropolitan area is successfully ministering in a popular contemporary style. It's called "varieties of gifts."

CHAPTER 6

Proclamation and Response

✝

INTRODUCTION

The Scriptures are opened to the people through the reading of lessons, preaching, witnessing, music, or other arts and media. Interspersed may be psalms, anthems, and hymns. Responses to God's Word include acts of commitment and faith with offerings of concerns, prayers, gifts, and service for the world and for one another. (*UMH* 2; *BOW* 15)

That is the way the Basic Pattern of Worship describes the second major division of the service, entitled "Proclamation and Response."

It is the Christian descendant of the synagogue service that Jesus knew. It is the time when God's Word is proclaimed to the people and the people make appropriate responses. It is the heart and core of the Service of the Word, and together with the Lord's Supper one of the twin foci of the complete Service of Word and Table.

The introduction to the Basic Pattern relates it to the Emmaus account:

As Jesus "opened the Scriptures" to them and caused their hearts to burn, so we hear the Scriptures opened to us and out of the burning of our hearts praise God. As they were faced

with a decision and responded by inviting Jesus to stay with
them, we can do likewise.   (*BOW* 14; Luke 24:25-29, 32)

From the earliest times, the reading and preaching of scripture have been at the heart of the Church's mission. The Basic
Pattern of Worship is designed to reassert the primacy of
scripture and the direct relation of the scriptures to preaching
and response.

The move from Entrance to Proclamation and Praise is a
dramatic turning point in the service, recalling the moment
when the two disciples on the road to Emmaus had finished
pouring out their hearts and Jesus began interpreting the
scriptures to them. Up to this point, while we have been aware
that we were responding to God's prior call, the emphasis has
been on our praise and prayer to God. Now the emphasis will
be on God's Word to us and our response to the Word.

An Order of Sunday Worship suggests that this turning
point be marked by a brief prayer that the Holy Spirit may
enlighten and empower the reading, preaching, hearing, and
doing of God's Word (*UMH* 3; *BOW* 22). This "prayer for
illumination" is a heritage from the Reformed tradition, to
which United Brethren cofounder Philip Otterbein belonged. It may take various forms, which the commentary
(*BOW* 22) describes. It may be combined with the opening
prayer and form a direct bridge from the singing of praise to
the proclamation of the Word. It is the counterpart in the
Service of the Word to the invocation of the Holy Spirit in the
Great Thanksgiving at the Service of the Table.

This prayer is more appropriate at the beginning of the
whole sequence of reading and preaching the Word than
immediately before the sermon. It is not just the preaching
but the reading, preaching, hearing, and doing of God's Word
that we are praying the Holy Spirit to enlighten and empower.

If this prayer is not prayed in unison, there is much to be
said for letting a layperson lead it. The pastor feels upheld by
the prayers of the laity. Since the point of this prayer is so clear
and direct, this is one of the easiest forms of congregational

prayer for laypersons to pray extemporaneously if they would rather do this than read a prayer. One congregation that had rarely used laypersons to lead prayer in the Sunday service began asking a different layperson each Sunday to lead this prayer and soon discovered that they had dozens of members, including youth, who were glad to lead the congregation in this prayer and most of whom prayed extemporaneously.

SCRIPTURE

Two or three Scripture readings should be used. If there are not Old Testament, Epistle, and Gospel readings at each service, care should be taken that over a period of time the people hear representative readings from each. (*UMH* 4)

More scripture is being read in United Methodist services than was the case a generation ago. This is because the primacy of scripture is being reasserted among United Methodists, and because it is evident that if the Bible is to exert its proper authority in the church the people need to know the stories and teachings that it contains. Since we live in a culture that is for the most part biblically illiterate, the only scripture that many people will hear is what they hear in church. We saw above (p. 49) that the early American Methodists set out to evangelize the nation with a pattern of worship that included the reading of two full chapters from scripture at each Sunday morning service. While the letter of that pattern may have been rigid, we are seeking to recover its spirit.

If a generous amount of scripture is to be "opened" to the people, it needs to be done well. The Bible is not boring, and it must not be read so badly that it sounds boring. Those who read scripture in worship should practice these readings, just as surely as choirs should rehearse anthems.

In many congregations one or more of the scripture lessons are read by a layperson. This follows ancient custom and is one of the ways laypersons can effectively share in the leadership of worship. Some laypersons are already highly effective readers, and others can become so through training. Richard Ward's booklet *Reading Scripture Aloud*, listed under Additional Resources, is a helpful resource. Many certified lay speakers serve as readers. By their careful preparation of the reading and by their sense of the importance of their ministry, readers can make the reading of scripture among the high points of the service. They should be allowed time and opportunity to prepare, and their ministry should be recognized and honored. It is both fair to all segments of the congregation and also more interesting and effective if the readers chosen over a period of time represent, in fair proportions, women and men, youth and young adults as well as middle and older adults, perhaps even older children, and whatever ethnic and cultural variety is in the congregation. The lay reader often sits in the congregation until time for the reading and then comes forward. This is a way of involving the congregation more closely in the reading and not separating the reader from family or from the rest of the congregation.

When scripture is read, the visual impact as well as the sound is important. Reading from a large pulpit Bible that all the people can see underscores the importance of scripture. In some congregations the Bible is brought in as part of the opening procession, placed on the pulpit, and opened at the beginning of the proclamation of the Word. When this Bible remains open in front of the preacher during the sermon, it emphasizes visually that the sermon comes from the Bible. On the other hand, to read the Bible from a (smaller) lectern rather than from the (larger) pulpit and then walk away from the Bible to the pulpit to preach sends the wrong visual message. Keeping a large Bible open on the Lord's Table and then never reading from it likewise sends the wrong visual message. During the service the place for a pulpit Bible is on the pulpit—open, read from, and preached!

Special thought should be given to the words used to introduce and close the reading of scripture. Suggestions for such words are given in the *Book of Worship* (23). An introductory comment explaining the setting of a reading is often appropriate, but it should be very brief and to the point.

The Scriptures can often be effectively opened to the people in ways other than solo reading. In some congregations the people are encouraged to follow a reading silently in pew Bibles or in their own Bibles. Pew Bibles also enable congregations to read a lesson in unison or in some responsive or antiphonal pattern. Two or more readers may do a dramatic reading from scripture; this can be highly effective with narrative passages as well as with dialogue. Many Bible stories can be acted out in a drama. Some Bible stories—the book of Esther, for instance—may lend themselves better to retelling, perhaps in the first person, than to straight reading. The retelling can be done in such a way that it is also the preaching.

Other arts may also enhance the words of scripture. Readings may be accompanied by sacred dance, visuals, or instrumental music. A passage that has been effectively and memorably set to music, such as one of those in Handel's *Messiah,* may be sung by a choir or soloist. In some situations film or video is feasible and effective.

What scripture should be read? In answering this question, three principles are basic:

1) Over a period of time the congregation needs to hear and learn the story and teachings of the whole Bible. It is not good enough for pastors to "ride their hobbyhorses." The people are spiritually malnourished if they hear only the scriptures that the pastor is familiar with or likes.

2) In this overall coverage of the Bible the centrality of Jesus Christ and of the basic gospel message needs to be evident.

3) The life situations and needs of the people at worship are important in selecting scripture as well as in preaching. A particular scripture may be especially timely and relevant on a particular Sunday. Of course, what people want to hear is not necessarily what they need to hear.

The historic practice of following a lectionary, or regular cycle of scripture readings, has much to commend it. The ecumenical Revised Common Lectionary found in the *Book of Worship* (227-37) includes for each Sunday in a three-year cycle a first reading (usually from the Old Testament), a second reading from some part of the New Testament other than the Gospels, and a reading from one of the four Gospels. This lectionary is the result of the work of a great many persons of many denominations. It was widely used in various earlier versions for over twenty years before the present revision was published ecumenically in 1992 and included that same year in the *Book of Worship*. A wealth of biblical interpretation, preaching resources, and other worship suggestions keyed to this lectionary is readily available. A great many pastors in The United Methodist Church and other denominations use this lectionary, and in many communities groups of pastors using the lectionary meet regularly together to share ideas for their forthcoming sermons. Many pastors inform their congregations in advance what the scripture readings will be so that the people can read them at home and be better prepared for the Sunday service. In many congregations one or more Sunday school classes or midweek groups study the lectionary scriptures for the same reason.[26]

The lectionary is not the only way of providing a full and balanced coverage of the Bible. Some pastors systematically preach through the Bible by some other plan they have discovered or devised. A pastor may wish to share with the worship planning team, worship commission, or congregation what plan she or he uses or wishes to use.

Use of the lectionary is not an all-or-nothing matter. Some pastors use the lectionary as their starting point and then feel free to substitute other scripture readings as circumstances in the life of the congregation warrant. Pastors may use the lectionary at some times of the Christian Year but not at others. If you and your congregation use the lectionary regularly, it is important to remember that it is a valuable resource, an excellent tool, a means to an end—but not an end in itself. Do not be enslaved to it. There may be good reason to omit a lectionary reading and to read and preach from a passage of scripture not in the lectionary or appointed for some other time in the three-year cycle. Your congregation may need to hear a passage such as John 7:53–8:11 even though it is not in the lectionary.

The lectionary can be used with adaptations. A reading may be shortened or lengthened. When the lectionary suggests a single brief reading from Jonah, several persons might present a fast-paced dramatic reading of the whole brief book. More of the story of Joseph in Genesis 37 and 39–50 can be told by the use of drama. Not only may there be two readings instead of all three, but there are times when even one may be enough. A Bible story such as just mentioned may take long enough to read, dramatize, or retell that no other readings are feasible at that service.

However the scriptures are selected, they are basic to the planning of the whole service. One of the great advantages of following the lectionary is that this makes it much easier for the pastor, musicians, and others to plan harmoniously as far ahead as desired. If the lectionary is not followed, the scripture readings should be decided upon by the pastor (or by the preacher if someone else will be preaching) and shared with other planners far enough in advance to permit the selection of appropriate music and other acts of worship. Then the continuing teamwork can be much easier and more efficient.

This does not mean that a service needs to be narrowly thematic. Congregations come to a service with a wide variety of needs, and there may be good reason for acts of worship that are not particularly related to the scriptures of the day. This is particularly true of the praises and prayers that precede the reading of the scriptures. What the service needs is not so much thematic unity as harmony among the acts of worship and a sequence of acts that makes sense.

SCRIPTURAL PRAISE

The Basic Pattern states that "interspersed [with scripture readings] may be psalms, anthems, and hymns." A Service of

Word and Table I (*UMH* 6-7, *BOW* 34) illustrates two ways in which this may be done. When we include the acts of worship in brackets we see the full ecumenical pattern embodied in the lectionary. When we exclude the bracketed acts we see a simpler pattern. In both patterns there is a rhythm of proclamation and response that illustrates the call-and-response pattern that is so fundamental to our worship in general. God's call comes to us through the reading of scripture, and we respond with acts of praise.

FULL PATTERN		SIMPLER PATTERN	
call	*response*	*call*	*response*
Scripture		Scripture	
	Psalm		Hymn or Song
Scripture		Scripture	
	Hymn or Song		
Gospel			

After the first reading, a psalm or psalm portions may be sung or spoken as an Act of Praise, the people standing. See *UMH* 735-862 and the lectionary for suggested psalms on [BOW] 227-37. An anthem based on the psalm is also appropriate. Before the final reading, a hymn or song related to the scriptures of the day, or an alleluia, may be sung. Because in the reading of the four Gospels we are addressed by the words of Christ and experience this as an encounter with the living Christ, many Christians prefer to stand and greet Christ with an **Alleluia!** except during Lent (see *UMH* 78, 186, 486, and the other alleluias suggested under "Acclamations" on [*BOW*] 19) and remain standing for the reading of the Gospel as an act of respect for the Christ who is addressing us.   (*BOW* 23)

Both acts of praise should be related to the scriptures being read. The psalms in the lectionary were chosen for the lectionary as appropriate responses to the first reading. The hymn or song between readings should be related to the message of the preceding or following reading. If a reading that follows is from the Gospels, the people may stand for the singing of the hymn and remain standing for the Gospel.

An "alleluia" is a greeting to the living Christ, whose words we are about to hear. If the congregation stands for the reading of the Gospel, it should be made clear that this is in no way a negative reflection on our reverence for God's Word in other books of the Bible. In all scripture and throughout our worship we are encountering the living God. The return to singing Alleluia! on Easter (Notice all the alleluias in our Easter hymns and liturgies!) adds drama to that peak day in the Christian calendar.

The use of an appropriate psalm or psalm portion as an act of praise is an ancient Jewish and Christian practice. When we praise God with a psalm, as with all praise, it is appropriate to follow the biblical custom of standing (see p. 90). Psalms used as praise function differently from readings and should not be considered substitutes for a reading from the Old Testament.

The Psalter in the hymnal (735-862) makes it possible to praise God with a psalm in various ways. The preface to the Psalter (736-37) is a helpful introduction to using the Psalter as praise. A fuller introduction is found in chapter 7 of *The Worship Resources of The United Methodist Hymnal.*[27]

We are in an exciting time during which the psalms are being rediscovered as praise and prayer. They are breathtakingly honest and powerful in their expression of the whole range of human feelings, and the prayers and praises we compose are usually guarded and bland by comparison. When we speak the psalms responsively (leader and people) or antiphonally (right side, left side) we feel their power.

The psalms are even more effective when we follow the biblical injunction to "sing praises with a psalm" (Ps. 47:7), as large segments of the church (including Luther, Calvin, and the Wesleys) have recognized through the centuries. The hymnal offers some imaginative ways for United Methodists to begin singing the psalms. Dwight W. Vogel's booklet, *Your Ministry of Singing the Psalms,* offers further help.

Three problems over the years have led many worshipers to resist praising God with psalms. (1) We were so trained to be "on our good behavior" when praying that we shrink from the honesty with which the psalms express every human feeling, acceptable or unacceptable. (2) It is hard for some persons to identify with the repeated references to Israel and things specific to the world of ancient Israel. (3) The most accurate English translations of the Hebrew in which the psalms are written cannot by their very nature be set to the kind of metrical hymn tunes United Methodists traditionally have sung in church. Metrical paraphrases of the psalms such as *UMH* 136 and 138 have helped, but they have to take such liberties with the words of the psalms that their truthfulness and power is compromised.

Fortunately, the situation is changing. (1) Christians are increasingly aware that we do not please God by being less than fully candid in prayer. We are not fooling God, only ourselves. If we want God to help us grow, we first need to acknowledge where we are now. (2) Christians are rediscovering and reclaiming our heritage from ancient Israel. (3) Christians are increasingly learning to sing psalms in a wide variety of musical styles that modern Americans can appreciate. What is in the hymnal is only a beginning. Keep on the lookout for the new psalm resources from many publishers that keep coming out, and keep trying those that seem most promising for your congregation.

SERMON

"One or more of the scripture readings is interpreted and proclaimed" (*BOW* 23). On the road to Emmaus, Jesus opened the scriptures to the two disciples and "interpreted to them the things about himself in all the scriptures" (Luke 24:27, 32). The verb we translate "interpreted" was used in New Testament times to refer to the preaching and teaching done in synagogue services, and that verb is still appropriate for Christian preaching today.

Jesus not only knew the scriptures, he had sensitively watched and listened as the disciples poured out their hearts (Luke 24:17-24). He then interpreted the scriptures to them in ways that spoke specifically to their needs. The effective preacher today is also a sensitive pastor who has been watching and listening and knows the needs of the people.

Opening the scriptures was a necessary part of the process by which the risen Christ encountered those two disciples and brought them into a new relationship with him. The preacher's task, week after week, is to bring persons to a new or renewed encounter and relationship with the risen Christ by interpreting and proclaiming Christ to them "in all the scriptures."

The reading and preaching of scripture are so closely related that the ancient and ecumenical practice of preaching the sermon immediately after the last scripture reading is strongly recommended. The practice so common in recent generations of placing pastoral prayer, announcements, offering, and hymn between the reading and preaching of scripture has had the effect of discouraging effective biblical preaching.

We cannot interpret "all the scriptures" in one sermon. That is why we need the cycle of the Christian Year. That is why we need either a lectionary or some other plan to interpret and proclaim the story and teachings of the whole Bible.

For that matter, it is often not feasible in one sermon to interpret all three scripture readings suggested for that day in the lectionary. During the Advent, Christmas, and Lenten seasons and on Easter, Pentecost, and certain other Sundays in the Christian Year, the readings are linked and a sermon may well be linked to all of them. At other times, trying to preach on all the readings would produce a disjointed, confusing sermon.

It is often best to preach on only one of the scriptures that are read. This is particularly likely to be true through the summer and fall months when the first reading, second reading, and Gospel are each going on its own cycle through three different books or sections of the Bible. There is much to be said for preaching consistently through one of these cycles during this half of each year. Thus in the summer and fall of Year C of the three-year cycle a pastor might preach through the Gospel of Luke. Three years later, when Year C came up again, that pastor might preach the cycle formed by the first readings. Three years later the pastor might preach from the second readings. This gives the pastor a nine-year cycle of summer and fall preaching texts.

In some Christian traditions the sermon is always expected to be based on the Gospel that has been read. Some lectionary-based preaching resources reflect that assumption. But United Methodists, together with most Protestants, do not see our preaching as limited to four books of the Bible.

Preaching can also be based on the psalm for the Sunday. While psalms are prayer and praise, they also are filled with preachable teachings and insights. Many preachers, for instance, have given effective verse-by-verse expositions of the succession of images in Psalm 23.

While there is much to be said for the ancient and ecumenical order of the readings, "the sequence of readings may be ordered so that the sermon is immediately preceded by the primary text to be preached" (*BOW* 22).

Some pastors are concerned that the needs of the people or the great issues that face our society and our world today will not be adequately dealt with if preaching is from scripture. This is a concern that we must take seriously, since there is no excuse for preaching what is irrelevant or insensitive to the life situation and needs of the congregation and the world. We must acknowledge that much preaching upon biblical texts has indeed been irrelevant and insensitive.

But the Bible *is* relevant to the whole range of our human needs, although our biblical illiteracy and limited imaginations may keep us from recognizing and effectively communicating its relevance. If this were not the case, we could hardly affirm the authority of scripture as we do. Our challenge is to discover and successfully communicate the Bible's relevance to human needs.

A pastor who preached a series of sermons on David from the lectionary scriptures through the summer of Year B reported this comment from a member of the congregation: "Since you showed me what David had to deal with as a king, I see for the first time how the Bible can help me function as a corporate executive." Another pastor might have preached from those same scriptures and left that same executive thinking, "I didn't come to church to find out what happened to the Jebusites." Being able to connect the world of the Bible, the world of the preacher, and the world of the people who hear the sermon is what makes the difference.

Biblical preaching can take many forms. Verse-by-verse or scene-by-scene preaching through a biblical passage can often be extremely effective but is far from being the only way for the imaginative preacher to interpret and proclaim the scriptures. A preacher can also, for instance, begin by describing a present-day life situation and then work back to the relevance of a scripture that was read or dramatized before the sermon. Sermon construction and preaching have been the focus of many books, and a full discussion is beyond the scope of this book. The important point here is that what has been said about the relationship between scripture and preaching should be seen not as confining the preacher to a particular form but as a challenge to the imagination.

Preachers who follow the lectionary sometimes wonder what to do on a Sunday when a situation in the congregation or an unexpected event in the community or the world is on everyone's mind and clearly needs to be addressed in the sermon. One option is to depart from the lectionary, read scripture that is relevant to what is on the minds and hearts of the people, and preach from that scripture. Another option is to deal with the situation or event in some part of the service other than the sermon. But first the preacher might well take another, more imaginative look at the lectionary scriptures. It is amazing how often a lectionary reading proves to be just right for an unexpected occasion, as countless preachers can testify.

Preaching is fully as important on Sundays when the Lord's Supper is celebrated as on other occasions. The omission of preaching on communion Sundays violates the unity of Word and Sacrament. A short sermon can be fully as important and effective as a long one and should not be called a "sermonette" or "meditation."

It is not necessary to preach on the subject of the Lord's Supper every time it is celebrated. Any aspect of the gospel can be preached in such a way that it leads naturally to the celebration of Holy Communion, since the Lord's Supper is a celebration of the entire gospel. In fact, where misunderstanding of the Lord's Supper is causing persons to stay away on communion Sundays, it may be well to preach about Holy Communion on one or more Sundays when it is not being celebrated, so that those whose misunderstandings need to be cleared up will more likely be present.

Some have suggested that services ought to pair scripture readings with modern readings as "the ancient word" and "the modern word." Such a pattern obscures the difference in kind that the church sees between scripture and all other writings and the unique place of scripture as the primary source and criterion for Christian doctrine.

There is, however, another way of looking at the issue. "The modern word" is the sermon. And yes, God can speak through modern writings just as surely as through modern preachers. Quotations and readings from ancient or modern authors and poets have been part of sermons from time immemorial. Sermons have often ended with a poem, as in the old three-points-and-a-poem pattern. They can just as well begin with a modern reading, which can help interpret the scripture or describe a life situation with which the scripture and sermon deal. If the reading is linked with the sermon rather than equated with scripture, the unique place of scripture remains clear.

The sermon is often strengthened by being conceived in flexible and imaginative terms. First person presentations where the preacher assumes the role of a biblical character, two persons preaching in dialogue, accompaniment of preaching by visuals or music, and use of objects in preaching are among the possibilities. Lay speaking, lay witnessing, or a musical presentation such as a cantata that proclaims the Word can on occasion supplement, or even be, the sermon for the day.

Drama is increasingly popular in worship and can serve any of several purposes. As was noted above, scripture passages can be dramatized. Also, a very brief drama can present a modern "life situation" and be the introduction to a sermon that deals with that situation in the light of scripture that has been read. On occasion a longer drama may itself be the sermon for the day.

Flexibility and imagination are particularly important as pastors increasingly welcome and recognize children in the worshiping congregation. Setting aside a time earlier in the service when the pastor or some other person talks specifically with children (children's sermon, children's story, moments with children) is a step toward full recognition of children in worship. A fuller recognition and involvement of children in worship comes when the sermon itself is preached in such a way that children as well as adults are interested and benefit. Perhaps the pastor who observes, "the adults get more out of my children's story than they do out of the sermon," should begin bringing to the sermon some of the imagination and creativity that has made the children's story so effective.

Imagination and creativity can also help involve youth and others who are now left out:

> Children, youth, and adults should hear and respond to the Proclamation of the Word. The sermon should communicate effectively with as wide a range of ages and stages of faith development as possible. (*BOW* 23)

RESPONSE TO THE WORD

Preaching is a call in search of a response. It is worship and evangelism in partnership. Responses to the proclamation of the Word can take many forms, some, but only some, of which are listed in the hymnal (4) and *Book of Worship* (24).

The call-and-response nature of our worship—the alternation of God's call and our response—is like a complex of rhythms in several tempos, or like a pattern of waves of several lengths and frequencies.

Call

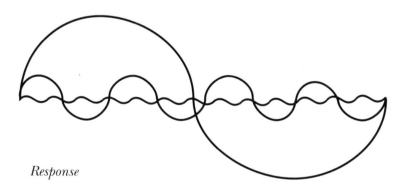

Response

This takes place throughout the service but is perhaps most clearly seen in the relationship of Proclamation and Response.

1) An immediate "short wave, high frequency" alternation of call and response occurs constantly during the entire service, including the sermon.

This is most obvious when persons in the congregation spontaneously respond with "amen," "praise God," applause, or other words or sounds during the sermon. Sometimes these responses are in turn a call to the preacher such as "preach" or "bring it home." As the preaching gains momentum, this call-and-response may go from being spoken to being intoned or sung.

This practice is common in African American worship and occurs in a variety of ways in many other congregations as well. Some preaching styles lend themselves to such responses, and others do not. Congregations to whom such responses come naturally will sense whether a particular preacher would appreciate and be helped by audible responses or whether they would throw the preacher off stride. Such a call-and-response pattern involves the congregation in the preaching and gives them added ownership of it.

While such practices cannot be forced on a congregation to whom they would be uncongenial, even normally reserved congregations sometimes respond audibly during the sermon. Some of the congregations that have started in recent years to applaud during worship will now occasionally applaud even during the sermon. One pastor recalls preaching to a usually reserved congregation about hypocrites, dramatically asking, "Who's the first person a hypocrite usually fools?" and being surprised but pleased to hear people all over the congregation saying, "Himself." A visiting preacher begins a sermon with, "It's Friday (pause), **but Sunday's coming!**" and periodically during the sermon repeats those words with increasing emphasis and growing congregational participation until at the end even that staid congregation hears a dramatic, "It's Friday," and shouts back, **"but Sunday's coming!"**

Even in the most reserved congregation there is constant call-and-response during the sermon. Not only do the people respond to what they hear with inward thoughts and feelings, they also express themselves, probably more than they realize. The people's posture, the nodding or shaking of their heads, their smiles and frowns, the looks in their eyes, their visible struggles against tears and laughter, all speak volumes. Preachers consciously or unconsciously read the body language of the congregation. They may also hear muttered comments not meant for their ears or guess the content of a whispered remark.

Preaching is more dependent upon such constant interaction with the congregation than many persons realize. Sermons often receive significant midcourse corrections as preachers perceive that their message is not getting through, or is meeting resistance, or is boring the congregation. The immediate thoughts and feelings of the people that give rise to their constant audible and visible feedback is also a foundation upon which their later responses to the Word can be based.

2) Long-term, "long wave" responses to the proclamation of the Word occur during the days that follow, as people take the proclamation of the Word to heart and seek to live by it. This is ultimately the level on which the proclamation seeks a response. But changed lives are more likely to happen if what is going on in the hearts of the congregation during the sermon can be expressed in some definite outward public response following the sermon.

3) That brings us to the time in the service following the sermon that An Order of Worship calls "Response to the Word" (*UMH* 4; *BOW* 24), described in the Basic Pattern as "acts of commitment and faith." In the rhythm of worship the sermon as a whole constitutes a call that seeks an immediate response in the form of one or more acts of commitment and

faith. We might think of these acts as the "medium wave" response to the Word that helps people move from their immediate good impulses during the sermon to long-term commitment in the days ahead. We may also think of it as a brief rehearsal for the difficult process of long-term commitment.

On the other hand, if people simply walk out of church after the sermon without doing anything to affirm their commitment to what has been proclaimed, then they have missed an opportunity to do something that would strengthen them as they go back to the difficulties of being Christians in their daily world.

Preachers often end their sermons with the call, "Let us pray," and then offer a short prayer that expresses the hoped-for response. Ideally, the whole congregation silently joins in this prayer and makes it their own by adding a personal amen. The danger is that this prayer will be experienced as simply an extension of the sermon and a solo act of the preacher. To move from such a prayer directly to the dismissal with blessing (benediction) is a grossly inadequate response to the Word.

The *Book of Worship* (24) urges that after the sermon there should be an invitation to Christian discipleship followed by an appropriate hymn of invitation (call) or response. Many sermons have a character and structure such that they naturally end with an invitation to Christian discipleship. If a sermon leads to a brief prayer, the invitation can follow the prayer. This invitation and the hymn that follows combine to form a bridge between the time of Proclamation (call) and the time of Response.

When no one comes forward during that hymn it often turns out that the hymn has been the only response to the sermon in that service. This is at best a minimal act of faith and commitment. Often it is clearly inadequate, particularly if the hymn is more of an invitation than a response of commitment and faith. If the invitation is given in such a way that those who are already church members can assume, "This invitation doesn't apply to me," then most of the congregation may leave the service without having made a clear act of commitment and faith. Certainly "the doors of the church are open" to new members, but it is also true that the proclamation of the Word calls for a response of commitment and faith from the whole congregation.

The *Book of Worship* (24) suggests that following the hymn a wide variety of additional responses to the Word may be appropriate. These specific suggestions deserve careful consideration by planners of congregational worship, and they do not exhaust the possibilities. They take into account the diversity of United Methodist congregations and the fact that acts of commitment and faith can be made in different heart languages and styles and for different specific purposes.

If persons come forward for a first commitment to Christ, they may not be ready for immediate baptism or confirmation. We cannot assume in modern American society that everyone who comes to church knows what it means to be a Christian and would know what they were doing if they made an immediate act of commitment. It may be appropriate immediately to recognize and honor a first commitment and then enroll the person(s) in a preparatory group for baptism or confirmation.

Baptism, confirmation, reaffirmation of faith, reception into The United Methodist Church, and reception into a local congregation are all acts of the highest importance that involve the commitment and faith not only of the individuals who come forward but also of the whole congregation. Since the people who come forward may be requesting various acts and combinations of acts of commitment and faith, it is easy for pastors to feel confused and in need of guidance. Pastors should be thoroughly familiar with the resources relating to these services not only in the hymnal (32-54) but also in the *Book of Worship* (81-114, 585-90). The *Book of Worship* adds important additional options to what is in the hymnal and contains very carefully written explanations of what these acts mean and how each act or combination of acts may be done.

Installations and recognitions of persons or groups, ministries of healing or reconciliation, consecrations or dedications of church buildings or furnishings, and commitments to specific actions or ministries are all provided for by resources in the *Book of Worship*. There is much to be said for planning as many of these as feasible during the course of a year. Imaginative planners of worship can discern additional possibilities beyond those suggested in the *Book of Worship*.

A time for silent reflection or spoken expressions from the congregation may be appropriate in the light of what has been read and preached that day. One congregation provides opportunity every Sunday for spoken responses from the congregation and finds great spiritual power in those moments. This can be a prime opportunity for lay witnessing and other movings of the Spirit.

The Apostles' Creed or another affirmation of faith gives the whole congregation an opportunity to make an act of commitment and faith at this point in the service. While affirmations of faith have been made at various points in United Methodist orders of worship, they are most naturally a response of commitment and faith to the Word. Use of the Apostles' Creed here is particularly appropriate because it was developed by the early church as the baptismal profession of faith, has historically been associated with baptism, and is included to this day in services of the Baptismal Covenant. There is no point in using the creed twice in one service. It is confusing to use the creed earlier in the service except when it will be used in the Baptismal Covenant, particularly if it is not known in advance whether there will be a baptism or confirmation. On Sundays when there is no Baptismal Covenant service, use of the Apostles' Creed at the same point in the service is a powerful reminder and reaffirmation of the Baptismal Covenant.

Everyone in the congregation should in one way or another be challenged and invited to an appropriate act of commitment and faith and given the opportunity to make such an act. In most congregations there are likely to be many services where no one comes forward to make an individual act of commitment or faith. Fears of personal and congregational disappointment on such days—perhaps fears of rejection or failure—make some pastors hesitant to give an invitation unless they know of someone who plans to respond. But such hesitation is needless. Whether or not there are additions to church membership at a given service, the congregation and its members can always make responses of commitment and faith. Perhaps their highest form of response is prayer, as we shall now see.

CONCERNS AND PRAYERS

No congregational worship service is complete without a time in which the joys and concerns of the congregation and the needs of the world are offered to God in prayers of thanksgiving, petitions, and intercession. This may be done in various ways, which are described in the *Book of Worship* (24-25).

Traditionally this has most often been done in United Methodist Sunday morning services in a pastoral prayer, in which the pastor composes and offers a prayer gathering up the concerns of the church and of the world. The congregation should then make this prayer their own by singing or saying amen or some other prayer response (see *BOW* 25).

Throughout American Methodist history there have been warnings and other evidences that pastoral prayers were too long and boring. They have often been abstract and general prayers for whole categories of people, and pastors have often fallen into the habit of repeating certain glib phrases Sunday after Sunday. Pastors have been afraid that if they named individuals they would be criticized for neglecting to name other individuals. If the people pray with their eyes closed there is loss of eye contact and the people's attention span is further shortened. Yet if the pastoral prayer is kept short it is likely to be all the more inadequate in dealing with the people's joys and concerns.

An adaptation of the pastoral prayer that has become very common in recent years is to invite and gather specific prayer requests in advance. In this way anyone has a chance to suggest a specific joy or concern, naming names; and the pastor has less fear of forgetting something or someone. This can be done in various ways, depending on the size of the congregation and the acoustics of the sanctuary.

In many congregations, even some fairly large ones, prayer concerns are now volunteered live from the congregation immediately before the prayer itself. The pastor, or someone else, then incorporates these concerns into the prayer that follows. This can add great vitality to the service if the sanctuary is such that anyone can speak up from wherever they are seated and be heard. Sometimes it works better if the pastor listens to the concern and summarizes it into the microphone. Aisle microphones or usher-passed cordless mikes are possible but usually awkward.

In most larger congregations, and some smaller ones, it is more feasible to invite and gather written prayer concerns. These can be submitted by mail or in person to the church office during the week or written on prayer request sheets posted strategically near the church or sanctuary entrances. They can be written on cards or slips of paper that are dropped into one or more prayer concern boxes as people are entering or collected by ushers earlier in the service. A supply of cards can be placed beside the boxes or in the pew racks. While written prayer concerns lack some of the impact of concerns expressed live, they have the advantage of giving the pastor or some lay volunteer(s) a chance to sort through, group, and condense the prayer concerns in advance.

One traditional alternative to a pastoral prayer is a litany of intercession and petition such as *BOW* 495, which is a shorter modern version of the Great Litany that John Wesley used and commended to the American Methodists. Its finely crafted language can say a great deal in remarkably few words. Repeated use of easily memorized response lines such as "Lord, in your mercy, **hear our prayer**," followed by silent prayer, enable the congregation to participate and stay alert without requiring that they have the text of the prayer in front of them.

Two variations of the litany pattern are increasingly popular in United Methodist services. In a congregation of any size a leader (not always the pastor these days) may pray a series of brief thanksgivings, intercessions, and petitions, each of which is followed by a congregational response such as "Lord, hear our prayer" or "Lord, in your mercy, **hear our prayer**." In smaller congregations, members of the congregation may volunteer these prayers from where they are seated, to each of which the congregation adds its response. In either case the congregational response may be sung (*BOW* 24).

Other traditional alternatives include bidding prayers and a sequence of short prayers, of which there are numerous examples in the *Book of Worship* (25). Additional short prayers can easily be composed by pastors using the classic collect form (*BOW* 447).

Tongsung Kido (*BOW* 446) is a form of congregational prayer where all pray their own prayers aloud at the same time. It is popular in Korean congregations and has long been known in segments of traditional American Methodism as well.

Prior to the prayers, whatever form they take, the choir or congregation may sing an invitation to prayer, and persons who wish to do so may be invited to kneel at the communion rail.

This time of concerns and prayers can occur at different points in the service. As mentioned above (p. 91) it can be part of the Entrance, as it was in early American Methodism. More recently it has often been between the scripture readings and the sermon—perhaps the worst possible location, where it breaks the continuity between the written and the preached Word.

There are, however, strong reasons to recommend the historic and ecumenical practice—found in the services described by Justin Martyr in A.D. 155 (see p. 38)—of placing these concerns and prayers after the sermon as a response to the Word.

1) Thanksgivings, intercessions, and petitions can better be made after the proclamation of the Word has motivated the people to be more aware of—and caring about—the joys and needs of the world and of the church.

2) Prayer is the most important and powerful immediate response that we can make to God's Word. An extensive and powerful proclamation of the Word calls for an extensive and powerful response by the whole congregation, centering in prayer. To limit prayer largely to the first part of the service— important as opening prayers are—fails to do justice to the crucial importance of prayer in worship and takes away what for many persons could be their chief immediate response to the Word.

3) When individuals have made acts of commitment and faith during the responses to the Word that have just taken place, it is important that the congregation immediately pray for and with them. This placement of the concerns and prayers gives the congregation the opportunity to do just that. These prayers are a bridge between the responses of commitment and faith these persons have just made and their long-term responses in the form of changed lives. They are also a bridge for the whole congregation between the faith they have just affirmed and their service in the world during the coming week.

INVITATION-CONFESSION-PARDON-PEACE-OFFERING

We have seen above (pp. 89-90) that confession and pardon can be either a form of opening prayer or a response to the Word. The fact that persons and congregations are likely to be more sensitive to their personal and corporate sin after the Word is proclaimed is a major consideration in favor of its being a response to the Word. It is particularly traditional and appropriate here when the Lord's Supper is celebrated.

Wherever confession and pardon are placed, they gain added meaning and power when placed within a larger sequence: invitation, confession, pardon, peace, and offering. This sequence is so scriptural and powerful that significant meaning is lost when it is broken up. It is possible to make this whole sequence the conclusion of the Entrance as an adaptation of the option discussed on page 91, but the sequence has most often been kept intact at this later point in the service. Here, when the Lord's Supper follows, this sequence serves as a bridge between the Service of the Word, where it functions as a Response, and the Service of the Table, for which it is a preparation. Let us look at this sequence in detail.

1) The *invitation* expresses Christ's loving invitation to repent of our sin, live in peace with one another, and (if the Lord's Supper follows) to join him at his table. If the Lord's Supper follows, two model invitation texts are found in *UMH* (7, 26). If the Lord's Supper does not follow, the invitation might be simply, "Let us confess our sin before God and one another."

2) The *confession* acknowledges our sinfulness, not only as individuals but as a church and as participants in the wider society, and prays that as a forgiven people we may grow in the spirit of Christ. It can be spoken or sung in a variety of ways (see *BOW* 20). It is followed by a time of silent prayer as people seek to make personal what has been prayed corporately.

3) The *declaration of pardon or words of assurance* declares God's pardoning and empowering love. Some act of pardon or assurance should always follow a prayer of confession, though it may take various forms (see *BOW* 20, 25-26).

The leader may be either an ordained minister or a lay worship leader (*BOW* 20). In United Methodist understanding of the priesthood of the whole body of believers, hearing one another's confessions and declaring God's pardon to one another is a mutual ministry of the whole body (1 Pet. 2:5, 9; James 5:16; John 20:22-23). There are often good reasons for leadership here by an ordained representative of the whole church, but in any case the leader needs this ministry as surely as the rest of the people do.

In the form found in A Service of Word and Table I (*UMH* 8; *BOW* 35) and II (*UMH* 12) the people return the declaration of pardon to the leader. They say: "In the name of Jesus Christ, *you* are forgiven," emphasizing the word *you* to make it clear that they are speaking to the leader. Then the leader joins the people in saying: "Glory to God. Amen."

Because of the close relationship of confession and pardon with healing (Matt. 9:1-8; Mark 2:1-12; Luke 5:17-26; James 5:14-16), they also have an important place in healing services and prayers (*BOW* 613-29).

4) The *peace.* Having made or renewed peace with God, the people may offer one another signs of reconciliation and love. In asking for God's forgiveness, we must be willing to forgive one another (Matt. 6:9-15; Luke 11:2-4). If God has forgiven us, we must then be willing to forgive others (Matt. 18:21-35; Eph. 4:31-32). Exchanging the peace after confession and pardon is a sign of reconciliation, peace, and love with one another.

In many instances, exchanging the peace will be primarily a gesture of love and blessing rather than reconciliation. This is perfectly appropriate when there is no history of conflict or estrangement.

But sometimes exchanging the peace will to a significant degree express desire or gratitude for reconciliation. Persons at this time may make their way to someone else in the congregation and take an initiative toward reconciliation with that person. Persons may be celebrating an accomplished reconciliation.

Whatever may be primarily in the hearts of those who exchange the peace, the word peace in this context is a translation of the biblical Hebrew word *shalom,* which is not a negative term for absence of conflict but means positive and comprehensive well-being. Since our peace is the gift of God's grace through Jesus Christ, it is not simply our peace but the peace of Christ that we are offering one another. Exchanging the peace is based on the New Testament Christian practice ("a holy kiss," "a kiss of love") mentioned in Romans 16:16; 1 Corinthians 16:20; 2 Corinthians 13:12; 1 Thessalonians 5:26; and 1 Peter 5:14.

This exchange of the peace may be done in various ways, and the statement in *BOW* 26 deserves careful study. Depending on the seating arrangement, cultural customs, and the degree of intimacy perceived as authentic for the people, it may be a simple handshake, a clasping of both hands, an embrace, or a kiss. If words such as those suggested in the *Book of Worship* seem too formal, they may be informal and spontaneous. They may be as simple as "peace," followed by a response of "peace" or "amen." The invitation to exchange the peace may include an invitation to stand, and most persons are likely to exchange the peace while standing; but there should be sensitivity to those who are unable to stand or who prefer to remain seated. The intensity and significance of the peace may vary from time to time, and differences of temperament and conviction should be respected.

However it is done, it is important not to confuse this act with the ritual of friendship or welcoming of visitors (see pp. 83, 91-92), which serves an important but quite different function in the service.

5) Placing the *offering* immediately after the exchange of the peace calls to mind Jesus' words: "When you are offering your gift at the altar, if you remember that your brother or sister has something against you, leave your gift there before the altar and go; first be reconciled to your brother or sister, and then come and offer your gift" (Matt. 5:23-24). The offering may be introduced by words such as: "As forgiven and

reconciled people, let us offer ourselves and our gifts to God" (*UMH* 8, 23; *BOW* 36).

There tends to be a good deal of ceremony connected with the offering in United Methodist congregations. Ushers may come forward at the beginning of the offering to receive the offering plates from the pastor. After the ushers have received the offering from the congregation, they may ceremonially bring it forward and present it at the Lord's table. The pastor may offer a prayer at one or the other of these times.

Offerings of praise may accompany the offerings of money. A hymn, a psalm, an anthem, or instrumental music may be offered as the offerings are being received from the congregation, or between the receiving of the offering and its presentation. A doxology or some other musical response may be sung as the offering is being presented. The *Book of Worship* (26-27) makes specific musical suggestions.

The offering may include much more than money, as the statement in *BOW* 26 explains; but given the importance of money in our society, the symbolism of our money offerings as acts of worship should not be underestimated. This act is more than collecting money needed to support the congregation's and denomination's ministries. It can be a symbol of our larger offering to God of ourselves and all that we have, to be used as God wills.

Underlying this offering is the doctrine of stewardship affirmed in the United Methodist Confession of Faith:

> We believe God is the owner of all things and that the individual holding of property is lawful and is a sacred trust under God. Private property is to be used for the manifestation of Christian love and liberality, and to support the Church's mission in the world. All forms of property, whether private, corporate or public, are to be held in solemn trust and used responsibly for human good and under the sovereignty of God. (*Discipline* 1992, Article XV, p. 70)

We are managers (stewards), not owners, of ourselves and all that we have. As such, we are accountable to God for the management of what God owns and has entrusted to us.

This understanding is expressed constantly throughout Jesus' teachings. Luke 12:42-48 is one of many instances. In fact, more than half of Jesus' teachings relate to the use of money and other property.

Under the sovereignty of God, human good is thoroughly interconnected with the good of all the rest of God's creation. During the course of the year this can be celebrated in a variety of ways such as harvest offerings or Thanksgiving displays or the blessing of animals (*BOW* 608-10). This is one of the meanings signified by reverently bringing forward or uncovering at this time the fruits of the earth (bread and wine) to be used in the Lord's Supper, as suggested in the *Book of Worship* (26).

While, as we have seen, United Methodist worship is primarily descended from ancient Jewish synagogue and family worship, the offering is the act of worship most clearly related to ancient Jewish Temple worship with its sacrificial offerings. We have seen above (p. 34) that the New Testament makes a place for Christian sacrificial offerings as acts of worship, provided they are seen as grateful responses to God's full, perfect, and sufficient self-offering in Christ, and not as attempts to placate God or buy God's favor.

Many congregations have experienced conflict over the placement of the offering in the order of worship and the particular way in which it is done. Because of the involvement of the congregation in giving money at this time, and because of the special roles of the ushers and musicians, many people feel a high degree of ownership in having the offering done in what to them is the accustomed manner. Many a pastor has tried to make changes in the offering and been surprised at how strong the resistance was. Any changes should be made with great caution, consulting in advance with the persons and groups involved and carefully explaining the changes to the congregation.

But while the offering may be received earlier in the service, there are strong reasons for receiving it here. Its significance as an offering (an act of commitment in response to the Word, a preparation for the Lord's Supper, part of the invitation-confession-pardon-peace-offering sequence) will be much more evident if it is here. If it is earlier it is more likely to be perceived as a collection or an intermission in the service. If it is at the end of the Entrance it is perceived by many persons as too early, and if it is between the scripture reading and the sermon it breaks the continuity between the written and preached Word. Some congregations receive the offering here when the Lord's Supper is celebrated and earlier in the service when it is not celebrated, but changing the position of the offering back and forth like that is confusing.

Wherever in the service the offering occurs, and however its symbolism is perceived, it should be linked with ministries to those outside the congregation and especially the poor. "The collection for the saints" requested by Paul from the churches in Corinth and Galatia when they gathered "on the first day of every week" was for the needy Christians in Jerusalem (1 Cor. 16:1-4). Persecuted congregations in the second century received an offering each week for the poor. In some United Methodist congregations it is the custom whenever the Lord's Supper is celebrated to leave a special offering at the communion rail for benevolences or for the pastor's discretionary fund for the needy. One United Methodist congregation today devotes 40 percent of its budget to ministries to the poor in its own inner-city neighborhood and more than another 10 percent of its budget to ministries elsewhere in the world outside the congregation.

That brings us to the Lord's Supper.

CHAPTER 7

Thanksgiving and Communion

✝

SERVICES WITHOUT COMMUNION

Several dozen United Methodist congregations today follow Wesley's advice and celebrate the Lord's Supper at the main service every Lord's Day, and probably several hundred others celebrate it at some service each week. The great majority of United Methodist congregations celebrate the Lord's Supper monthly, quarterly, or on key days in the Christian Year. This means that most United Methodist Sunday services are services of the Word but not services of Word and Table.

As we shall see below, the Lord's Supper consists of two basic elements: *Thanksgiving* (for God's mighty acts in Jesus Christ) and *Holy Communion* (with God and one another through sharing the bread and cup). A Service of the Word cannot provide communion through sharing the bread and cup, but it can include thanksgiving. For this reason, the Basic Pattern of Worship provides that "in services without communion, thanks are given for God's mighty acts in Jesus Christ."

The words most crucially needed but missing from the Service of the Word as we have discussed it to date are: (1) thanksgiving for God's mighty acts in Jesus Christ that have made us the Body of Christ and given us communion with the living God in the power of the Holy Spirit, and (2) the Lord's Prayer, which is the supreme model of Christian prayer. Some would add a third: a time of silence to contemplate and experience the communion that we can have with God, even without the Lord's Supper.

Suppose we are invited to someone's house and have a wonderful evening of conversation. We talk about many things and have a rich sharing. But something crucial is missing if before leaving we do not thank our host(s) for their hospitality. It is an appropriate time to pledge again our friendship.

If we come to church at God's invitation and have a wonderful time of sharing with God and one another, something crucial is also missing if before leaving we do not give thanks to God. To be sure, we have already made provision in the Service of the Word for general prayers of praise and for including thanksgiving for our specific recent joys in the concerns and prayers. But what about the things God has done to make life with its greatest joys and ultimate hopes possible in the first place? These we too easily take for granted; we must not let our gratitude for them go unexpressed. And it is an appropriate time to pledge again our loyalty and friendship to God.

How this is to be done is deliberately left open and flexible in the Basic Pattern. Just *how* we do this is less important than *that* we do this. It can be done in various ways. Some claim that this is done when we recite a creed or affirmation of faith, but what we do then is really not the same. For one thing, these are not prayers thanking God; they are more like testimonies. Also, many affirmations of faith deal more in timeless truths about God than in the story of God's mighty acts.

This thanksgiving could be done as part of the opening praise and prayers or as part of the concerns and prayers, but in either of those places experience shows that the kind of thanksgiving we are referring to tends to get neglected. It easily gets lost or at least passed over too lightly amid a multitude of other prayer concerns. As with a visit to a friend, we can express our deepest gratitude and pledge anew our friendship during opening greetings or in the course of conversation about what has happened lately, but it usually seems more natural to save such expressions until toward the end of the visit.

An Order of Worship (*BOW* 27) recommends that it be after the presentation of the gifts in the offering, and this suggestion has much to commend it. The gifts being presented are outward and visible tokens of our inward gratitude and dedication to the God who is everything to us, but what we are doing needs to be expressed in words as well. Pastors commonly do this by offering a prayer when the gifts are presented, but offertory prayers have generally been too narrowly focused to express adequately what we are doing. The prayer texts printed in the *Book of Worship* (27, 550-55) give thanks for God's mighty acts in Jesus Christ and also express in words what we have done in the offering.

If the offering has been received before the proclamation of the Word, this prayer of thanksgiving might well follow whatever other responses to the Word have been made. It could, for instance, appropriately follow a baptism, confirmation, reception by transfer, or other act in response to an invitation to Christian discipleship.

What could follow such a prayer of thanksgiving and consecration? Only what the *Book of Worship* suggests: the supreme model of Christian prayer, the Lord's Prayer. It may be spoken or sung by the congregation, but it should not be taken away from the people by a choir or soloist. Surely this takes the Service of the Word as high as words can go.

Beyond that? "A time of silence may follow the Lord's Prayer" (*BOW* 27). In this holy moment our spirits can soar beyond the range of words to silent communion with God. It may suggest and echo the sharing (*koinonia*) of the bread and cup in Holy Communion, and we may hunger and thirst for the next Lord's Supper. Then we reenter the world of words for the Sending Forth.

In one congregation the practice when the Lord's Supper was not celebrated was for the prayer of thanksgiving to use most of the text and responses of the Great Thanksgiving prayed at their Holy Communion services. Only Jesus' words instituting the Lord's Supper and the invocation of the Holy Spirit upon the bread and cup were omitted. Then followed the Lord's Prayer, after which there was a long period of silence, referred to as "silent communion," during which many persons came forward and silently joined the pastor in kneeling at the communion rail. The silence was gently broken by the organ introduction to the closing hymn, and those who were kneeling could take their time about returning to their seats.

THE SERVICE OF THE TABLE

When the Lord's Supper *is* celebrated, we have seen that the invitation-confession-pardon-peace-offering sequence is a bridge from the Service of the Word to the Service of the Table. Now we are in the Service of the Table, which the Basic Pattern of Worship describes as a fourfold action:

In services with communion, the actions of Jesus in the Upper
    Room are reenacted:
taking the bread and cup,
giving thanks over the bread and cup,
breaking the bread, and
giving the bread and cup.

We have made the transition from a service primarily of words to a service primarily of actions. In the bridge sequence the invitation, confession, and pardon are still primarily words, while the peace and offering are primarily actions. Of the four acts that constitute the Service of the Table, three (taking, breaking, and giving) are primarily actions, and only one (giving thanks, or blessing) is primarily words.

We have already seen these four actions of *taking, blessing* (giving thanks), *breaking,* and *giving* in the ministry of Jesus (pp. 33, 35) as he fed the hungry multitudes, instituted the Lord's Supper, and ate with the disciples at Emmaus. Since the first and third of these actions are brief and preliminary to the second and fourth, we may group these actions into two pairs: (1) taking the bread and cup and giving thanks over them, and (2) breaking the bread and giving the bread and cup to one another. These two steps may be referred to simply as *Thanksgiving* and *Communion.*

The Bible makes it clear that the Lord's Supper is a *meal.* It is breaking bread and drinking from the cup with the living, risen Jesus Christ and with our sisters and brothers in Christ at the Lord's Table. The four basic actions are the actions of a host at a meal, and the risen Christ is hosting us just as surely as when he was recognized by the disciples in those first resurrection meals.

We have seen that since the time of the early Christians this holy meal has usually been a token meal of bread and wine rather than a full-course meal, but this does not change the fact that it is a meal. Our daily lives are full of token meals that fulfill the communal purposes of eating and drinking together on occasions when we neither need nor want to eat a full meal. If I visit someone in the middle of the afternoon, for instance, they are likely to offer me token food or drink. Refreshments at meetings, such as a coffee break or coffee and dessert, often fulfill a similar communal purpose.

Eating and drinking together is a very basic, primordial human act of bonding with other human beings. It has multiple meanings that are taken very seriously across the range of human cultures. Even in a secular society such as ours, it is accompanied by all kinds of customs and taboos. The Lord's Supper is a very special and holy meal, but we can understand its special and holy character better if we keep in mind that it is a meal.

What does the Lord's Supper mean? It means everything that eating and drinking together means, and incomparably more. Thousands of books have been written through the centuries and throughout the world on its many meanings. Several of these are listed under Additional Resources. If what it means could fully be put into words, then the holy meal itself might be unnecessary and we could content ourselves with the words. Words can only point in the direction of what can be conveyed only by the experience itself, and even the experience grows and changes as we do. One facet of meaning will be most important to one person, another facet to another person.

This sacred act is called by a variety of names, each of which highlights some facet of meaning but no one of which does full justice to it. Calling it the *Lord's Supper* highlights the fact that it is a meal hosted by our Lord. *Holy Communion* highlights the holiness and intimacy of the union of Christ and his Body (the Church) that this act creates and expresses. *Eucharist* highlights the spirit of joyous thanksgiving that permeates it. *Breaking of Bread* highlights its earthy simplicity. Calling it a *sacrament*, from the Latin term for a soldier's pledge of allegiance, tells us that it is both Christ's pledge of commitment to us and our pledge of commitment to Christ and his church. Calling it an *ordinance* affirms that it was instituted and ordained for us by Christ.

We celebrate in *remembrance* of Christ, but as we saw above (p. 33) the New Testament word we are translating is stronger than our English word. It means bringing Christ from the past into present reality. Past and present meet at the Lord's Table.

Yes, and they meet the future there, too. We eat and drink there "until he comes" in final victory (1 Cor. 11:26). This token food and drink, like the token food and drink served by a host before the dinner is ready, is both a foretaste of heaven for each of us and also a foretaste of the messianic feast, God's ultimate victory banquet.

We could go on and on with additional meanings. Each is a point of view from which we can see part of the whole meaning of this sacred act. Those who find meaning in one viewpoint need not argue with those who find meaning in another.

Ultimately, the communion *(koinonia)* that we have with God and one another in Jesus Christ is a *mystery*. The Bible speaks of "the mystery of the gospel" (Eph. 6:19), "the mystery of the faith" (1 Tim. 3:9), "the mystery of our religion" (1 Tim. 3:16), "the mystery of Christ" (Col. 4:3), "the mystery of God" (Rev. 10:7), and "this mystery, which is Christ in you, the hope of glory" (Col. 1:27). We are "stewards of God's mysteries" (1 Cor. 4:1).

When a pastor or other ordained minister presides at this holy meal in the name of Christ, she or he is a steward to whom is entrusted a sacred responsibility to pass on a treasure that goes beyond the understanding of any of us. If God reveals to someone sitting in the congregation something that the pastor did not intend or was not aware of, that's all right. None of us is so wise as to have plumbed the depths of the mystery.

On the other hand, the mystery of the gospel is revealed even to young children—*especially* to young children, if we remember Jesus' words (Mark 10:13-16). A small child eating and drinking at the Lord's Supper already connects being fed with being loved and feels included at the meal rather than excluded. God reveals facets of the mystery of the gospel to children at whatever their stage of development as they share in this holy meal. Do they fully understand what they are doing? Of course not, and neither do you and I! Recognizing that young children are part of Christ's family, United Methodists increasingly welcome them to Christ's family meal.

In fact, our adult theories and explanations are sometimes barriers to God's continuing revelation of the mystery to us. If we once learned some way of explaining the Lord's Supper, we need to remember that our understanding of this sacred mystery did not begin with that explanation and should not end with it. On the other hand, we may find it hard to receive Holy Communion, or even stay away, because some interpretation we once heard is incredible or offensive or simply doesn't make sense. Perhaps that interpretation should be put aside in favor of one better suited to our present capacity for understanding or in favor of more openness to the mystery of it all.

Many United Methodists have stayed away from the Lord's Supper over the years because they misinterpreted Paul's warning:

> Whoever, therefore, eats the bread or drinks the cup of the Lord in an unworthy manner will be answerable for the body and blood of the Lord. . . . For all who eat and drink without discerning the body, eat and drink judgment against themselves. (1 Cor. 11:27, 29)

This passage has been so often misunderstood that pastors should be careful to preach on its true meaning.

Reading the whole passage (verses 17-34), we discover that Paul was referring to a situation in the church at Corinth where persons brought their own food and drink to what was still a full meal at that time. Some were eating and drinking to excess and refusing to share with others who had brought nothing and were going hungry. Those selfish persons were obviously communing "in an unworthy manner." They were eating and drinking "without discerning the body" by being oblivious to the hungry people right there in front of them who were Christ's body the Church. They were shutting themselves off from the Christ who was in "the least of these" (Matt. 25:31-46).

Paul's warning has nothing to do with the level on which we can intellectually understand the sacred mystery. Just as Christ's invitation includes children as well as persons of all ages who are mentally limited, we can be glad that his invitation includes us, regardless of our level of understanding.

Paul's warning also has nothing to do with our present level of moral development, providing we come to the Lord's Table open to letting Christ raise us, whether we are the worst sinner or the greatest saint, from our present level to something higher. Receiving Holy Communion in a worthy manner does *not* mean receiving because we are worthy. The only way any of us is worthy is through God's free gift in Christ, and to come to the Lord's Table because we thought we had earned the right to be there would in itself be an unworthy motive. Christ has always been known as one who liked to eat with sinners (Luke 15:2), and he still does.

Pastors should also be sensitive to other barriers that keep people from the Lord's Table.

Persons with disabilities should not be prevented from receiving Holy Communion. The church building should be free of barriers to their attending and coming forward. Whatever assistance is needed should be provided, including bringing Communion to persons where they are seated if they cannot come forward. If they are able and wish to come forward, they should feel welcome to receive sitting in a wheelchair or front seat as well as standing or kneeling.

Holy Communion should regularly be brought to persons who are hospitalized, institutionalized, homebound, or otherwise desirous of Communion but unable to attend services. While the pastor or associate pastor should engage in this ministry whenever feasible, "ordained elders may select and train lay members with appropriate words and actions to immediately deliver the consecrated Holy Communion elements to members confined at home, in a nursing home, or in a hospital" (*Discipline* 1992, Par. 1217.9, p. 503). A Service of Word and Table V (*BOW* 51-53) is designed for either clergy or lay members to use with persons who are sick or homebound. It is adaptable to a variety of situations and should be studied and thought through carefully in advance.

If people are staying away on Holy Communion Sundays for reasons such as the length of the service or the style of the "ritual," serious consideration should be given to making changes or adding an alternative style of Lord's Supper celebration. Ways of doing this will be suggested below. One United Methodist congregation that has flourished for many years celebrating the Lord's Supper at both main services every Sunday has been careful to provide people with a choice of two different lengths and styles of service, each of which is designed to be in the heart language of those who attend. They recently added a still different style of Lord's Supper service on Saturday evenings.

Often a congregation is divided as to how often they wish to celebrate the Lord's Supper. If there are persons who wish Holy Communion more frequently than does the rest of the congregation, there should be a way to provide for their needs. If a congregation has more than one weekly service, the Lord's Supper might be celebrated more often at one than at the other(s). A growing number of United Methodist congregations celebrate the Lord's Supper weekly at an early service, a Saturday or Sunday evening service, or a weekday service, while the main service remains a service of the Word. Another possibility for those who have attended the weekly Service of the Word and also wish Holy Communion is to gather them in the front of the sanctuary or in a smaller chapel a few minutes after the service and have simply a Service of the Table with them.

Pastors who wish to increase the frequency of celebrating the Lord's Supper at what is now simply a Service of the Word should be cautioned against hasty actions. The first priority should be to celebrate the Lord's Supper, whenever the congregation is accustomed to celebrating it, in such a way that the people come to *want* it more often. Then it's time to increase the frequency. One pastor shared with the Sunday school superintendent his pleasure that attendance had started going up rather than down on Holy Communion Sundays. The superintendent replied: "Don't you know, preacher? The word has gotten out that you preach better and do everything better on Communion Sundays."

How do we celebrate the Lord's Supper more effectively? Let's look at some possibilities, step-by-step.

THANKSGIVING

"*Taking* the bread and cup" and "*giving thanks* over the bread and cup" are the first two of the four actions of the

Lord's Supper as described in the Basic Pattern of Worship. Since taking the bread and cup is a brief act that leads directly into giving thanks over them, we may consider them together as *thanksgiving.*

The discussion of taking the bread and cup in the *Book of Worship* (27-28) contains much practical information that repays careful study. If the Communion bread and wine (grape juice) were not brought to the Lord's table at the time of the offering they should be brought there at this time. If they were not uncovered at the time of the offering, they should be uncovered and any wrappings removed at this time. If a chalice is to be used and the Communion wine has been in a pitcher or flagon, the wine is poured at this time into the chalice. All this should be done with a simple dignity and reverence that conveys to the congregation the sacred character of the sacrament.

The *Book of Worship* describes and encourages several recent and widespread reforms that represent a return to earliest Christian practice: (1) The pastor stands behind the Lord's Table, which is once again a freestanding table rather than an altar against the wall. (2) A large uncut loaf of bread, which later in the service is broken and distributed to the people, is once again used, rather than precut cubes or wafers or pellets. (3) A large common cup, called a chalice, is used, although drinking from the chalice is usually replaced by dipping the bread into the chalice. Grape juice continues to be substituted for wine, for the reasons stated in the *Book of Worship.*

The thanksgiving (blessing) over the bread and cup is called *The Great Thanksgiving.* United Methodists had inherited from the Church of England and from the medieval Roman Catholic Church the practice that this prayer was broken into fragments that were given such names as "sursum corda," "preface," "prayer of consecration," and "prayer of oblation." The result was a collection of prayers whose rationale was not clear and that were often referred to collectively as "the communion ritual." We have now restored this prayer to its New Testament and early Christian unity.

The New Testament, as we have seen, tells us that Jesus *blessed* (Matt. 14:19; 26:26; Mark 6:41; 8:7; 14:22; Luke 24:30; 1 Cor. 10:16) or *gave thanks* (Matt. 15:36; 26:27; Mark 8:6; 14:23; Luke 22:17, 19; John 6:11, 23; 1 Cor. 11:24) before meals, including the one at which the Lord's Supper was instituted. Ancient Jewish blessings blessed God, as in Psalm 103:1-5, recalling what God does that is related to the occasion for blessing. Jews also gave thanks to God for God's mighty works, as in Psalm 111. Christian tradition combines these dimensions of thanksgiving and blessing.

Today we give thanks (say a blessing) over our food and drink when it is brought to the table, before we begin the meal. The purpose, after blessing and thanking God for God's goodness and unmerited favor ("saying grace"), is not to make holy the fruits of the earth that God has already made holy by creation. They are so holy, in fact, that we refrain from eating them until we have invoked God's blessing. In the words of a familiar blessing, we pray God to "bless them to our use and us to your service."

We do this in a special way when we gave thanks (say a blessing) over the bread and cup before partaking of the Lord's Supper.

The Great Thanksgiving, together with the Lord's Prayer that immediately follows it, is the one part of the Service of the Table that is primarily words. As such, it is our primary means of expressing what we are doing and what we are petitioning God to do in the Lord's Supper, and it is crucial that it do so fully and accurately. It needs to be a prayer of the universal Church that is invisibly gathered around the Lord's Table. It also needs to be expressed in the heart language of the people visibly present, so that it can be truly their prayer, not just empty "ritual."

It is hard to compose a prayer that does all that. Some denominations require clergy to use a Great Thanksgiving prepared and approved for this purpose by denominational authorities. This shows concern for orthodox theology and for the universal church but risks leaving congregations without a Great Thanksgiving in language that is truly theirs. Other denominations allow complete freedom as to what if anything is prayed over the bread and cup. This allows pastors and congregations freedom to use their own heart language but risks errant theology and estrangement from the heritage of the universal church.

The United Methodist Church takes a middle course. It gives its pastors great freedom when they preside at the Lord's Supper, with all the risks that entails. But it also provides in the hymnal and *Book of Worship* carefully prepared and officially approved denominational resources for the Great Thanksgiving, without requiring that pastors use them. Several services of Word and Table are provided, with models and guidelines for praying the Great Thanksgiving in diverse ways. The guidelines in An Order of Sunday Worship (*BOW* 28) are especially important.

A Service of Word and Table I (*UMH* 6-11; *BOW* 33-39) is a fixed text, fully printed out in the hymnal so that the people can read through both the Service of the Word and the Service of the Table. Variable acts such as hymns and scripture readings can easily be announced. This service is convenient in that it requires a minimum of advance preparation and requires no bulletin. It suits those who feel at home reading acts of worship and having in front of them the text of what the pastor is reading. It is desirable to vary the prayers during the course of the year, but doing that is more awkward in this format. All this applies to the Great Thanksgiving in that service as well as to the rest of the service.

A Service of Word and Table II (*UMH* 12-15) continues the tradition in American Methodism since 1792 of a printed text for only the part of the service beginning with the invitation. The Great Thanksgiving is shorter, an abridgment of the text in Service I. As the introduction to this service in the *Book of Worship* (40) explains, it may be prayed as it stands or words suited to the day, season, or occasion may be added by the pastor at points marked with an asterisk. The pastor can easily do this by reading one of the seasonal Great Thanksgivings (*BOW* 54-77), all of which contain the entire text of the Great Thanksgiving in Service II with words added at the appropriate places. The added words may also be of the pastor's own selection or composition. In either case, the people simply follow Service II in the hymnal.

A Service of Word and Table III (*UMH* 15-16) is the simplest and most flexible of the services of Word and Table. Nothing but cue lines and congregational responses are printed out for the Great Thanksgiving. Since the essential parts of the prayer that the pastor leads are not printed out, the pastor must supply these in one of the ways suggested by the introduction to Service III in the *Book of Worship* (40).

Service III will feel less formal to many people. Many people prefer a style of worship with a minimum of reading. As the cue lines and congregational responses are used and become familiar, the congregation will feel at home with them and have less need to read them from the hymnal. There is room in this format for a high degree of variety and creativity.

The five musical settings for the Great Thanksgiving (*UMH* 17-25) and the introduction in the *Book of Worship* (40) make it easier and more effective than it has ever been before in our hymnals to sing the responses in the Great Thanksgiving. The pastor can use the Great Thanksgiving from Service I or II, or one of the seasonal or alternative Great Thanksgivings in the *Book of Worship*. The pastor can also compose or select a Great Thanksgiving if the necessary cue lines are included. When one of these settings is used, the service can be printed in the bulletin with just a line for the Great Thanksgiving: THE GREAT THANKSGIVING - Musical Setting C - Hymnal 20.

These settings are designed for the diverse needs of United Methodist congregations. The four printed with only the melody line should be sung in unison; full accompaniment is found in the accompanist's edition of the hymnal. Settings A and B are the simplest and best suited to congregations just beginning to sing these responses. Setting C will appeal because of its great beauty, especially when sung in four-part harmony. Setting D is in a minor key and is suited to more somber seasons and occasions such as Lent. Setting E, expansive and majestic but complex and demanding, will richly repay congregations willing to work at learning it.

A Service of Word and Table IV is a traditional text from the rituals of the former Methodist and Evangelical United Brethren churches. A text beginning with the invitation is found in the hymnal (26-31), and a complete text is found in the *Book of Worship* (41-50). These texts preserve the majestic sixteenth-century language style of *The Book of Common Prayer* that John Wesley used and loved. They tie us to several centuries of our Anglican and United Methodist past—a significant segment of the universal church. Using them continues to be a blessing for those United Methodists to whom they are precious. They have been lightly edited to keep them usable by contemporary United Methodists, most notably by gathering the fragmented prayers of the Holy Communion ritual together into a unified Great Thanksgiving.

Comparing the Great Thanksgiving in Service I (*UMH* 9-10) with the one in Service IV (*UMH* 27-30) we can see that significant reforms have taken place in the past generation.

The prayer in Service I uses what might be called a modern classical language style that is neither archaic like that of the prayer in Service IV nor blunt or trendy like some contemporary prayers.

The prayer in Service I has a three-part structure, each part ending with a congregational response. This structure, taken from some of the earliest known Christian Great Thanksgivings, is now widely used in other Christian denominations. Today it is an ideal framework for expressing a strong and balanced trinitarian theology. The whole prayer is addressed to God the Father, and its first part is praise and thanksgiving for creation and the covenant with Israel. The second part is thanksgiving for redemption through Jesus Christ and the

New (Baptismal) Covenant. The third part is a petition for the gifts and fruits of the Holy Spirit and an anticipation of final victory.

Joyous celebration of the whole range of God's mighty acts contrasts with the overwhelming preoccupation with Jesus' death that gave previous Holy Communion texts their funereal tone. We celebrate the joy of God's creation. We give thanks for the whole ministry and saving work of Jesus Christ. In the power and unity of the Holy Spirit, Holy Communion becomes not only a remembrance of the past but a resurrection meal with the living Christ and a foretaste of the heavenly feast.

There is a strong social dimension in this prayer. It gives thanks for the ministry of the prophets. It recalls Jesus' statement of his mission in Luke 4:18-19 and gives thanks that "he healed the sick, fed the hungry, and ate with sinners." It petitions that through the Holy Spirit "we may be for the world the body of Christ" and "one in ministry to all the world." The term "ministry" includes justice as well as service ministries. The term "the world" includes not only human beings but an ecological concern for the whole world.

Thanksgiving for the whole range of God's mighty acts can be still more comprehensive if the Great Thanksgiving can be varied during the course of the year. Traditionally this has been done by "proper prefaces" in what is now the first section of the Great Thanksgiving. Now the *Book of Worship* (54-77) provides a series of Great Thanksgivings with seasonal changes in any or all of the three sections of the prayer.

Three alternative Great Thanksgivings (*BOW* 52-53, 78-80) show still further possibilities. Two of them are brief, without congregational responses except for the final amen, and show ways of structuring a Great Thanksgiving when brevity is essential and congregational participation is not feasible.

These models do not exhaust the possibilities for a knowledgeable and creative pastor "giving thanks over the bread and cup." The outer limits of what constitutes an acceptable

Great Thanksgiving are a matter of considerable debate. But it may be helpful to add a few suggestions to the models and guidelines in the hymnal and *Book of Worship*.

First and foremost, by all means *give thanks* to God over the bread and cup before giving them to the congregation. It is astonishing how often United Methodist pastors do not do this. When they then begin giving the bread and cup at this holiest of meals, one is tempted to ask: "Aren't we going to have a blessing?"

Simply quoting to the congregation Jesus' words instituting the Lord's Supper is hardly a prayer of thanksgiving to God. Jesus' words are usually incorporated into the thanks given to God, where they are most appropriate indeed. In some traditions the Great Thanksgiving itself does not include Jesus' words, and they may be quoted outside the prayer as a warrant for celebrating the Lord's Supper. But, however it is done, this moment in the service calls for thanksgiving to God—a blessing that is more than simply Jesus' words of institution.

The three-part trinitarian structure may be followed without necessarily using the opening dialogue, cue lines, and congregational responses in Service III.

As the two brief Great Thanksgivings in the *Book of Worship* (52-53, 80) illustrate, there may be no congregational responses except the final amen.

The Great Thanksgiving may have a two-part structure of *thanksgiving* and *invocation*, in which "the pastor [1] gives thanks appropriate to the occasion, remembering God's acts of salvation and the institution of the Lord's Supper, and [2] invokes the present work of the Holy Spirit, concluding with praise to the Trinity" (*BOW* 28). There may or may not be a congregational response in the middle, at the end of the thanksgiving. It is, of course, fully as important in a two-part structure as in a three-part structure that there be a whole and balanced expression of trinitarian faith.

So far we have been focusing on the words of the Great Thanksgiving, but this prayer is more than words. We also give thanks with our body language. In biblical times and in the early church people stood for prayer (see p. 90), and the *Book of Worship* (28) recommends that both pastor and people be standing for the Great Thanksgiving. This is no time to kneel as if in confession; this is a time of joyous praise.

The Bible speaks of our hands as contributing to the body language of prayer. "I desire, then, that in every place the men should pray, lifting up holy hands" (1 Tim. 2:8). Psalms 28:2; 63:4; 134:2; 141:2 and Lamentations 2:19; 3:41 speak of lifting up hands in prayer. Solomon "spread out his hands to heaven" when he prayed (1 Kings 8:22).

The Great Thanksgiving texts in the *Book of Worship* make suggestions regarding the prayer language of the pastor's hands. When it is suggested that the pastor "may raise hands," there is no one and only "correct" way to do this, but the traditional way is to raise the hands to about shoulder height, with palms upturned and elbows bent at about a right angle, as in this drawing:

When the prayer is referring to the bread or the cup, it is suggested that the pastor's hands be held, palms down, over the bread or the cup as a focusing gesture. Alternatively, the pastor may touch or lift them.

Many pastors seem utterly unaware of how they look when they lead prayer with their eyes glued to a book they are holding in front of them at chest or even shoulder height. Of course, they may assume that everyone's eyes are closed, but they shouldn't take this for granted. Many people pray best with their eyes open, using their eyes as an aid to prayer.

Pastors are likely to ask, "How do I read the text if I can't hold the book or the bulletin?" One answer, of course, is to memorize the prayer or to pray extemporaneously. This is highly effective if done well, but it is difficult for many pastors and often done poorly.

Modern technology has come to the rescue. It is now easy to get a large print version of any Great Thanksgiving or other act of worship with an enlarging copier or by using word processing printed out in large type. These sheets can be laid flat on the communion table or, better yet, placed inside an attractive cover on a missal stand. It may not be long before the average pastor will be able to use something like a tele-prompter.

What could follow the Great Thanksgiving? By ancient tradition dating from the sixth century, it is that supreme model of Christian prayer, the Lord's Prayer. When the Lord's Supper is celebrated, as well as when it is not, the Lord's Prayer should be spoken or sung by the whole congregation and not taken away from the people by a choir or soloist. The pastor may introduce it with a sentence such as, "And now, with the confidence of children of God, let us pray: . . ." These words are appropriate because the Great Thanksgiving has just reminded the people of all God's mighty acts that have made us God's beloved children, and because they are about to address God as Father in the Lord's Prayer. The pastor may lead the Lord's Prayer with hands raised as in the Great Thanksgiving.

Since Methodists and Evangelical United Brethren used different translations of the Lord's Prayer ("trespasses" and "debts" respectively), and since an ecumenical translation ("sins") has come into wide use in the past generation, all three translations are printed out in the hymnal (894-96). The Lord's Prayer may also be sung from the hymnal (270-71). It is important to print in the bulletin the number in the hymnal of the version your congregation uses. Many persons, especially seekers, do not know the Lord's Prayer; and visitors will want to know which of the translations to use.

This is a good place to make a more general statement. Never assume that everyone in the congregation knows anything by memory. Always let them know how to look it up in the hymnal, or print it out in the bulletin, even if most of the congregation does know it by memory.

A final comment on the Lord's Prayer comes from the *Book of Worship* (29):

> This forms a bridge between the first pair of actions in Holy Communion (Thanksgiving) and the second pair (Communion). It is both the sublime climax of our thanksgiving to God and the verbal entrance into a communion with God that is holy beyond words.

COMMUNION

"*Breaking* the bread" and "*giving* the bread and cup" are the third and fourth actions of the Lord's Supper as described in the Basic Pattern of Worship. Since breaking the bread is a brief act that leads directly into giving the bread and cup, we may consider them together as *Communion*.

The *Book of Worship* (29) describes how breaking the bread is done, but some additional comments may be helpful. Using a single unbroken, uncut loaf of bread is a New Testament practice (1 Cor. 10:17) signifying that we are one body in

Christ. This practice is increasingly being restored in United Methodist congregations. Breaking the loaf into as many pieces as there are persons who will be assisting in its distribution is a practical way of beginning the giving of the bread to the people. Breaking the bread and raising the cup are also symbolic gestures inviting the people to come, eat, and drink.

While these acts may be done in silence or accompanied by various appropriate statements, the words of 1 Corinthians 10:16-17 printed in A Service of Word and Table I (*UMH* 11; *BOW* 39) are perhaps most frequently used at this time. The pastor holds up the whole loaf while saying, "Because there is one loaf, we, who are many, are one body, for we all partake of the one loaf." Then the pastor breaks the loaf while saying, "The bread which we break is a sharing in the body of Christ." Then the pastor lifts the cup while saying, "The cup over which we give thanks is a sharing in the blood of Christ." The pastor may then say words such as, "Come, the table is ready."

Giving the bread and cup is the fourth and final action of the Lord's Supper, the act to which all the others have been leading. The invitation expressed in breaking the bread and the response of the people as they come to the Lord's Table is the climactic call-and-response in the service, the clearest representation of God's ultimate call to the heavenly table and our gathering at the heavenly banquet. While feasting at the Lord's Table we go beyond call-and-response to a communion *(koinonia)* with God in Christ, with one another, with the church of all times and all places, and indeed with the whole creation. The meanings of the Lord's Supper discussed above (pp. 131-34) apply most particularly to this climactic act. The extensive discussion of this act in the *Book of Worship* (29-31) includes many insights and practical suggestions that are worth careful consideration.

It is a pity that planning for such a sublime moment has to attend to a host of practical details, but once again we are reminded that God (like the devil) is in the details.

A practical problem in many United Methodist congregations, especially larger ones, is the length of time it takes to serve everyone. This more than anything else can make the service uncomfortably long and is one of the major reasons some United Methodists stay away from Holy Communion. A congregation must find a solution to this problem before its members can be expected to want Communion more frequently.

One solution is to serve Communion to the people seated in the pews, who then serve one another as the bread and cups are passed along each pew. This effectively deals with the time problem but keeps the people passive and deprives them of the significant act of coming forward for Communion. Many persons, however, strongly prefer this way of receiving Communion. Some United Methodist congregations with more than one weekly service serve Communion in the pews at one service, while at the other service the people come forward. Some other United Methodist congregations always serve Communion in the pews.

In most United Methodist congregations the people come forward to receive Communion. Traditionally they have generally received Communion kneeling at a communion rail, a medieval Roman Catholic practice continued by the Church of England and passed on to us by John Wesley. In more and more United Methodist congregations today, the people come forward to a "communion station" and receive Communion standing.

Many United Methodists would be surprised to learn that there are numerous celebrations of the Lord's Supper at which literally thousands of people, very reverently and without any sense of haste, come forward and receive Communion in fifteen minutes or less. While a congregation that wishes to take thirty or forty-five minutes to serve the people has every right to do this, it is quite possible for a congregation of any size to come forward and receive Communion in fifteen minutes or less. It all depends on how it is done.

The most time-consuming way to serve Communion is to usher the people forward "by tables," each "table" simultaneously kneeling at the rail, eating the bread, drinking a cup, and returning to their seats after a brief meditation or "table dismissal." In addition to doubling the time spent in serving Communion, this practice dictates to the people how long they are to spend at the rail and fills those sublime moments with too many words.

If in addition the pieces of bread and the individual cups are spread out along the rail and the people are asked to serve themselves ("self-service communion"), the central symbolic significance of Communion is compromised:

> It is our custom to serve each person individually, while exchanging . . . words. . . . Serving one another acts out our faith that Christ is the giver of this holy meal and that we are receivers of Christ's grace.   (*BOW* 29-30)

The grace we have received from God we pass on to others as we serve one another. Various phrases may be used in the exchange of words, and this exchange should be as warm and personal as possible (*BOW* 29-30).

If takes less time and is less regimented if persons come and go freely at the rail, while those who are serving Communion move back and forth behind the rail. Ushers can still be helpful, moving from pew to pew in a way and at a pace that invites people to come forward but prevents a long lineup of persons waiting for a space at the rail. Persons can remain kneeling as long as they wish, holding out their hands until they have been served.

"Laypersons as well as other clergy may assist the pastor in giving the bread and cup" (*BOW* 29). Serving Communion can take less time without any sense of hurry if at least two persons, one ministering the bread and the other ministering the chalice or tray of cups, serve from behind the rail. When they move along the rail, the server of the bread should go first, immediately followed by the server of the cup(s). It works

best if the pastor or the more experienced server goes first
and serves the bread. It is that person who first senses and
responds to special situations—a shaking hand that needs
steadying, a small child who needs special help, a signal from
an usher to serve someone seated in a pew—and sets an
example for the server of the cup(s) to follow. When they have
moved the length of the rail, they should move promptly back
to the end of the rail where they started and begin serving
again. With larger congregations and longer rails it may be
wise to use more than one pair of servers, each serving a
designated segment of the rail.

In a similar way, persons can come forward and receive
Holy Communion while standing in front of what is known as
a *communion station*—a pair of servers, the first serving the
bread and the second the cup(s). There should be a communion station in the front of each aisle that people will be using
to come forward. The communion station(s) should be outside the communion rail (if there is one) and on the same
level as the congregation, not on a step or platform. If there
is a communion rail and there are people who wish to kneel
there once they have received the bread and cup, they may be
invited to do so for as long as they wish. If the people are given
individual cups, the empty cups may be left in the pews or in
appropriately placed baskets or trays.

The larger the congregation or sanctuary, the more communion stations may be needed. They may, for instance, be
halfway up long aisles or at the front of balcony aisles. There
seems to be no limit to the number of persons who can
reverently be served in this fashion in fifteen minutes or less.

Another way of giving the bread and cup is for the people
to stand in a circle around the Lord's Table or along the walls
around the sanctuary and pass the bread and cup around the
circle, each person serving the one next to them, with words
exchanged as the Spirit moves. This is especially effective in
smaller congregations or services. If desired, the congregation
may form this circle immediately after they have exchanged

the peace and informally left their offerings in some designated place, remaining in a circle through the entire Service of the Table and until the Going Forth.

However the distribution of the bread and cup is done, it begins as the pastor and other servers gather at the Lord's Table to receive the bread and cup(s) for distribution:

> It is traditional that the pastor receive the bread first and then serve those who are assisting in the giving of the bread and cup; but, if desired, the pastor and those assisting may receive last. One of those assisting may serve the pastor.   (*BOW* 30)

The suggestions in the *Book of Worship* (30-31) regarding singing while the bread and cup are given, what is done after the people have been served, what is done with the remaining bread and wine, and thanksgiving after Communion are well expressed and require no further comment here.

Giving the bread and cup is not only sublime in itself, it is a model for what is to happen in the moments and days ahead. Giving the bread and cup to the whole congregation not only signifies God's self-giving in Christ for the sake of the whole world, it also renews our identity as the Body of Christ for the sake of the world and is a means of grace for our ministry to all the world. As the bread and cup are sent forth from the Lord's Table to the congregation, so we are about to be sent forth into the wider world. Our fair and generous distribution of the bread and cup to the congregation models the distributive justice and compassion we are sent forth to practice with respect to all humanity. Our stewardship of God's gifts of bread and wine is a model for our stewardship both of the gospel and of all God's gifts, including the fruits and resources of the earth. As the bread and wine are now in us and part of us, so Christ is in us and we are part of the whole ecology of creation. We are now ready for the Sending Forth.

CHAPTER 8

Sending Forth

✝

HYMN OR SONG AND DISMISSAL WITH BLESSING

> Whether or not Holy Communion has been celebrated, the
> service concludes with a series of acts in which the congrega-
> tion stands and is sent forth to active ministry in the world.
>
> (*BOW* 31)

These acts should normally be brief. This is our reentry into
the world, for which our worship has equipped us. We can no
more remain indefinitely on the peak—"the high"—of worship experience than the disciples could remain on the Mount
of Transfiguration (Matt. 17:1-13; Mark 9:2-13; Luke 9:28-36).

"Facing the people, the leader declares God's blessing. The
hymn [or song] may precede or follow the blessing" (*UMH*
5). This can be done in many ways, a number of which are
suggested in the *Book of Worship* (31-32). Many congregations
have a theme song or chorus that they sing every week in
closing, perhaps joining hands.

What is commonly called the benediction is referred to in
the *Book of Worship* as the Dismissal with Blessing. It is just that:
both a dismissal and a blessing. It is a dis-missal (literally a
"forth-sending") of the people into their mission in the world.
And it is a blessing, given by the pastor in the name of the

triune God to the people, face-to-face. "If the closing hymn or song is a recessional in which the pastor joins, it should follow the dismissal with blessing" (*BOW* 32). This permits the pastor to give the dismissal with blessing to the people, face-to-face, from the front of the sanctuary. The suggestions previously given above regarding the processional apply to the recessional as well.

As mention of a recessional illustrates, actions as well as words send, or lead, us forth. Everything during this time is usually done with the congregation standing, which signifies that they are preparing to leave. Pastors usually accompany their words of blessing with a hand raised in a gesture of blessing, and sometimes the congregation joins hands at this time. One congregation for years has ended its 11:00 A.M. Easter service with a congregational procession out the door and through the neighborhood, led in some years by a saxophonist playing such tunes as "When the Saints Go Marching In."

GOING FORTH

"Like the Gathering, the Going Forth is an act of corporate worship as long as people are still with other people in the place of worship" (*BOW* 32). Furthermore, it is an important part of the service, just as the Gathering is.

As with the Gathering, congregations sometimes find themselves in controversy about what should or should not be expected during the Going Forth. And as with the Gathering, there is no one-size-fits-all solution. Indeed, the fact that such controversies arise is testimony to the importance of the Going Forth in the minds and hearts of the people. The *Book of Worship* (32) mentions four activities, one or more of which may be included in the Going Forth.

Many controversies have centered around the "organ or other instrumental voluntary, during which the people are free to go forth, remain standing quietly in place listening, or sit down to listen." This voluntary is a part of the worship, just as surely as is the music played or sung during the Gathering. The term "postlude," implying that the music is after (post) the service, is inadequate for the same reason that "prelude" is. It should be respected as a musical offering of worship to God and an aid to the people's worship.

But the overwhelming desire for immediate "informal greetings, conversation, and fellowship" before the friends or visitors they want to greet get away is also an important worship need. It often echoes the spirit of the peace. What was previously said about greeting visitors applies just as surely here as during the Gathering. There may be newly received members in the front of the sanctuary to be greeted by the congregation. For various reasons, it is even harder to insist, "Wait until you are outside the sanctuary," here than it is during the Gathering.

Some people need or wish to leave promptly, some visitors wish to remain anonymous, and some regular attenders want to be left alone. Sensitivity to who seems to want personal attention and who does not is important. The pastor of a large city church advises other pastors that during the Going Forth they should "always leave one door unguarded." In other words, don't station someone to greet people on the way out at every door.

One way of giving people a choice is to hold a coffee hour somewhere outside the sanctuary for those who wish to socialize. This has many advantages, but a warning must be given. Visitors who attend coffee hour are signaling that they want to meet people, and if the church members there are preoccupied with talking to their friends the visitor will experience that congregation as decidedly unfriendly. Special care should be taken to give a warm welcome to all coffee hour visitors. In any event, a coffee hour outside the sanctuary is not likely to keep people from talking in the sanctuary.

Some persons will choose to "remain standing quietly in place listening, or sit down to listen," to the music, but this cannot be forced on everyone. People are not likely to feel like sitting down after they have just been stood on their feet and been dismissed. After attending a worship service where the people were directed to do this, a professional dancer who was attending said, "That's bad choreography."

Knowing all this, many instrumentalists regard what they play at this time as "walking music." Such music is typically short, brisk, and upbeat. It can be an effective accompaniment to the Going Forth.

Of course, circumstances alter cases. During the Going Forth one Easter Sunday morning in a large and sophisticated United Methodist congregation with a magnificent organ, a virtuoso organist played one of the most spectacular works in the organ repertoire. Hundreds of people listened standing in place and then came forward and crowded around the organ console as if an evangelist had given an altar call—this in a congregation that would not have been caught dead responding to mass evangelism. Many people clearly regarded it as the climax of the service. But whatever one thinks of that as an act of worship, the fact is that most church musicians playing the instruments at their disposal could not have elicited such a response in their congregations if their lives had depended on it.

As the congregation scatters, their meeting for worship is over and their service begins in the wider world. In a larger sense, their worship continues in an ongoing, even if usually unconscious, communion with the living God through the risen Christ in the power of the Holy Spirit. Ultimately we are all part of the cosmic communion of creation with Creator. This communion links past, present, and future in an eternal now that is stronger than death. We are not yet ushered into the banquet hall for the ultimate feast, but the refreshments of our worship here and now have given us such a taste of it that heaven can wait until our service in the world is accomplished.

Notes

†

1. *The United Methodist Hymnal* (Nashville: The United Methodist Publishing House, 1989).

2. *The United Methodist Book of Worship* (Nashville: The United Methodist Publishing House, 1992).

3. Hickman, Hoyt L. (ed.); Saliers, Don E.; Stookey, Laurence Hull; White, James F., *The New Handbook of the Christian Year* (Nashville: Abingdon, 1992).

4. *The Book of Discipline* (Nashville: The United Methodist Publishing House, 1992).

5. A classic expression of this view of worship is the opening paragraph of Evelyn Underhill's *Worship* (New York: Harper & Brothers, 1937), p. 3. One might also expand upon the central thought of Sallie McFague's *The Body of God* (Minneapolis: Fortress, 1993) to suggest that as Christian worship is the communion of Christ with Christ's body the church, so ultimately the history of the universe is the communion of God with God's body the whole creation.

6. The discussion of worship as drama that follows is expanded and updated in its imagery from Søren Kierkegaard, *Purity of Heart,* part XII.

7. Norman Perrin, *The Resurrection According to Matthew, Mark, and Luke* (Philadelphia: Fortress, 1977), pp. 76-77.

8. For a comprehensive study of the history and varieties of Protestant worship, see James F. White, *Protestant Worship: Traditions in Transition* (Louisville: Westminster/John Knox, 1989).

9. Albert C. Outler, ed., *The Works of John Wesley,* vol. 3 (Nashville: Abingdon, 1986), pp. 427-39.

10. Ibid., p. 428.

11. These are included with extensive introductory material in J. Ernest Rattenbury, *The Eucharistic Hymns of John and Charles Wesley* (American edition edited by Timothy J. Crouch) (Cleveland: OSL Publications, 1990). Four Wesley eucharistic hymns are in *The United Methodist Hymnal* (1989), nos. 613, 616, 627, and 635.

12. Ibid., p. 2.

13. Most recently reprinted with introduction, notes, and commentary by James F. White as *John Wesley's Prayer Book: The Sunday Service of the Methodists in North America* (Cleveland: OSL Publications, 1991).

14. Ibid., p. 1.

Notes

15. Ibid., p. ii.
16. Ibid., p. iii.
17. *The Doctrines and Discipline of the Methodist Episcopal Church in America*, revised and approved at the General Conference held at Baltimore, Maryland, November 1792, 8th ed. (Philadelphia: Printed by Parry Hall, sold by John Dickins, 1792), pp. 40-41.
18. Ibid., pp. 228-33.
19. Samuel S. Hough, ed., *Christian Newcomer: His Life, Journal, and Achievements* (Dayton: Board of Administration, Church of the United Brethren in Christ, 1941). These sacramental meetings lasted from one to three days. The 35 one-day meetings were typically on a Sunday. In the 146 two-day and 24 three-day meetings the first day was entirely preaching, the Lord's Supper was administered on the second day, and often there was also a Love Feast on the second or third day. They were held in every month except January and February. These are much more frequent than the 58 camp meetings *Newcomer* records, most of which were in August and almost all of which were after the first authorized United Brethren camp meeting in 1815. His eloquent comments on these meetings well repay a reading of the entire journal.
20. For a comprehensive discussion of the African American worship heritage see Melva Wilson Costen, *African American Christian Worship* (Nashville: Abingdon, 1993).
21. *Minutes of Several Conversations Between the Rev. Thomas Coke, LL.D., The Rev. Francis Asbury and others, at a Conference Begun in Baltimore in the State of Maryland, on Monday, the 27th of December, in the Year 1784, Composing a Form of Discipline for the Ministers, Preachers, and Other Members of the Methodist Episcopal Church in America* (Philadelphia, 1785), p. 28, and later editions of the *Discipline*, quoting from Wesley's *Large Minutes* of 1780.
22. Wesley, *Sunday Service*, pp. 7-14.
23. Kierkegaard, *Purity of Heart*, chapter 12.
24. *The Book of Worship for Church and Home* (New York and Nashville: The Methodist Publishing House, 1945), pp. 1-2.
25. *The Cokesbury Worship Hymnal* (Nashville: Whitmore & Smith, 1938). Now published by Abingdon.
26. For full information about the history and development of the Revised Common Lectionary, together with the lectionary itself and all its ecumenical options, and with an index of the readings in their biblical order, see *The Revised Common Lectionary* (Nashville: Abingdon, 1992).
27. *The Worship Resources of The United Methodist Hymnal* (Nashville: Abingdon, 1989). Chapter 7 was written by Charles Michael Smith and Dwight W. Vogel. Hoyt L. Hickman was volume editor.
28. Dwight W. Vogel, *Your Ministry of Singing the Psalms* (Nashville: Discipleship Resources, 1991).

Additional Resources

✝

The United Methodist Hymnal: Book of United Methodist Worship. Nashville: The United Methodist Publishing House, 1989. Designed for use by every United Methodist congregation.

The United Methodist Book of Worship. Nashville: The United Methodist Publishing House, 1992. Essential for all who plan or lead worship in United Methodist congregations.

Guidelines for Leading Your Church: Worship 1993-1996. Nashville: Abingdon, 1992. How to organize and carry out the planning of congregational worship.

By Water and the Spirit: A Study of Baptism for United Methodists. Nashville: Cokesbury, 1993. A study guide.

The Revised Common Lectionary. Nashville: Abingdon, 1992. A comprehensive book about the Revised Common Lectionary.

Benedict, Daniel, Craig Kennet Miller. *Contemporary Worship for the 21st Century: Worship or Evangelism?* Nashville: Discipleship Resources, 1994. An examination of contemporary worship styles and the role of worship in reaching seekers.

Bowyer, O. Richard, Betty L. Hart, Charlotte A. Meade. *Prayer in the Black Tradition.* Nashville: The Upper Room, 1986. An excellent introduction.

Costen, Melva Wilson. *African American Christian Worship.* Nashville: Abingdon, 1993. An excellent introduction.

González, Justo, editor. *¡Alabadle! Hispanic Christian Worship.* Nashville: Abingdon, 1996.

Hickman, Hoyt L. *Your Ministry of Planning Worship Each Week.* Nashville: Discipleship Resources, 1988. A practical guide for planning services week by week.

——. *The Acolyte's Book.* Nashville: Abingdon, 1985. A training booklet for acolytes.

——. *United Methodist Altars.* Nashville: Abingdon, 1984. A manual for altar guilds.

——. *United Methodist Worship.* Nashville: Abingdon, 1991. A study book for laypersons.

——. *Workbook on Communion and Baptism.* Nashville: Discipleship Resources, 1990. A study book for laypersons.

——. *Your Ministry of Being a Communion Steward.* Nashville: Discipleship Resources, 1991. A training booklet.

——, editor, Don E. Saliers, Laurence Hull Stookey, James F. White. *The New Handbook of the Christian Year.* Nashville: Abingdon, 1992. A comprehensive book on the meaning and observance of the Christian Year.

Johnson, Kenneth M. *Ushering and Greeting.* Nashville: Discipleship Resources, 1989. A practical guide for church ushers and greeters.

Langford, Thomas A., III. *Blueprints for Worship.* Nashville: Abingdon, 1993. A user's guide to *The United Methodist Hymnal* and *The United Methodist Book of Worship.*

O'Donnell, Michael J. *Your Ministry of Being an Acolyte.* Nashville: Discipleship Resources, 1991. A training booklet for acolytes.

Phillips, Sara Webb and L. Edward. *Your Ministry of Leading Public Prayer.* Nashville: Discipleship Resources, 1992. Practical help for clergy and laypersons in leading prayer.

Stookey, Laurence Hull. *Baptism: Christ's Act in the Church.* Nashville: Abingdon, 1982. A comprehensive study of baptism.

——. *Eucharist: Christ's Feast with the Church.* Nashville: Abingdon, 1993. A comprehensive study of the Lord's Supper.

Vogel, Dwight W. *Your Ministry of Singing the Psalms.* Nashville: Discipleship Resources, 1991. Practical training in singing the psalms.

Ward, Richard. *Your Ministry of Reading Scripture Aloud.* Nashville: Discipleship Resources, 1989. Practical helps for those who read scripture in worship.

White, James F. and Susan J. White. *Church Architecture: Building and Renovating for Christian Worship.* Nashville: Abingdon, 1989. A comprehensive guide for designing or renovating sanctuaries or chapels.

White, James F. *A Brief History of Christian Worship.* Nashville: Abingdon, 1993. The best introductory book in its field.

———. *Introduction to Christian Worship: Revised Edition.* Nashville: Abingdon, 1990. A basic textbook.

———. *Protestant Worship: Traditions in Transition.* Louisville: Westminster/ John Knox, 1989. A study of the varieties of Protestant worship.

Willimon, William H. *Remember Who You Are.* Nashville: The Upper Room, 1980. A study book on baptism for laypersons.

———. *Sunday Dinner.* Nashville: The Upper Room, 1981. A study book on the Lord's Supper for laypersons.

———. *With Glad and Generous Hearts.* Nashville: The Upper Room, 1986. A study book on Sunday worship for laypersons.

Wiltse, David A. *Your Ministry of Designing the Worship Bulletin.* Nashville: Discipleship Resources, 1991. A booklet for pastors and church secretaries who design bulletins.

Young, Carlton R. *Companion to The United Methodist Hymnal.* Nashville: Abingdon, 1993. Everything you ever wanted to know about *The United Methodist Hymnal* and the hymns in it.